COOKBOOK

Austin Edition

Trailer Food Diaries

Tiffany Harelik

Serving up the American Dream one plate at a time!

Published by Trailer Food Diaries LLC
Austin, Texas
www.trailerfooddiaries.com

Distributed by Greenleaf Book Group LLC

For ordering information or special discounts for bulk purchases, please contact
Greenleaf Book Group LLC at PO Box 91869, Austin, TX 78709, 512.891.6100.

Design and composition by October Custom Publishing
Cover design by Tom Kirsch Design

Publisher's Cataloging-In-Publication Data
(Prepared by The Donohue Group, Inc.)

Harelik, Tiffany.
  Trailer food diaries cookbook. Austin edition / Tiffany Harelik. -- 1st ed.

  p. : ill. (chiefly col.) ; cm.

"Serving up the American dream one plate at a time."
Includes index.
ISBN: 978-0-9837911-0-2

  1. Street food--Texas--Austin. 2. Cooking--Texas--Austin. 3. Cooking, American--
Southwestern style. 4. Cookbooks. I. Title.

TX715.2.S69 H27 2011
641.59/764/31   2011937011

ISBN 13: 978-0-9837911-0-2

Part of the Tree Neutral® program, which offsets the number of trees consumed in
the production and printing of this book by taking proactive steps, such as planting
trees in direct proportion to the number of trees used: www.treeneutral.com

Printed in the United States of America on acid-free paper

12 13 14 15 16 10 9 8 7 6 5 4 3 2

First Edition

A bird doesn't doubt the wind.
This book is dedicated to anyone
who has ever taken a leap of faith.

Contents

Acknowledgments

The Trailer Food Diaries cookbook and projects

are dependent on many good people. I am grateful for my role in compiling and narrating and would like to acknowledge with deep appreciation the other characters in this cast. First, thank you Mom and Dad for patiently cheering me on when I quit my job to pursue a more passionate life. Thank you to my little girl, who came with me to many a trailer this year. Thank you to all the trailer food vendors for venturing creatively into your own passions. You are inspiring, and I love your food. Roy Spence, Charlie Jones, David Rockwood, thank you for believing in this project. Jenifer and John Martin, thank you for connecting me and coaching me. Maurine Winkley, thank you for being there every step of the way. All the founding ladies in the Gemini Moon Writers' Group (Deborah Mastellato, Kimberly Key, Connie Quillen, Mollie Staffa, Kriss Kovach), thank you for all the late nights in the salon and the saloon. Jason Claurer, thank you for helping me connect with the right people at the right time. To the independent design team, whom I never met in person until we were a year into this: Tom Kirsch (Tom Kirsch Design), and Torquil Dewar (October Custom Publishing), your countless hours have made all the difference in completing this project. To photographers Laurie Virkstis, Stefani Spandau, Sarah Wilson, Rudy Arocha, Bill Lanier, and all the photographers who submitted photos, thank you for your beautiful talent and contribution to this edition. Greenleaf Book Group, thank you for your enthusiasm and commitment to this book. Finally, thanks to everyone who has helped with *Trailer Food Diaries* in some capacity: Marla Camp, Sarah Loden, Adam Christians, Bob Makela, Keith Maitland, Lisa McWilliams, Bob Gentry, Terry and Brooke Heller, Archangel Gabriel, the farmers and gardeners who produce our trailer food, the staff at C3 Presents, GSD&M, and Greenleaf Book Group, and all others who contributed heart and time.

You are all inspiring; you all made this cookbook. It's my intention that it inspire others to live their dreams, or at the very least, make some good food in the process.

Introduction

My great-grandfather Haskell

came to the United States in the early 1900s and started his pursuit of the American dream with a mobile banana cart. As a Jew who had been living in an oppressive dark corner of Russia, he decided to take a leap of faith and get on a boat that would carry him to a place where he would be free. Once he arrived in Galveston, Texas, he was a pretty sad sight. As was common practice, the immigration officers changed his last name upon entry to the States. He didn't have a home, and he had no money, no family, or anything that resembled the life he knew in Eastern Europe. He didn't speak English. He didn't even have his family name.

What he did have was a dream. With his humble personality, along with dependability, he garnered the trust of a local banker who took a chance on this out-of-place character. He purchased a mobile food cart and began selling bananas for a penny each in Hamilton, Texas. Over time, the banana cart turned into a fruit stand. Eventually he opened five general stores throughout central Texas and sent back for his family in Russia. Haskell Harelik showed up for his life. He didn't give up.

Flash forward to 2009. In modest comparison with my great-grandfather's experience, I wasn't happy. I took a leap of faith and quit the eight-to-five world to embark on new territory. I had no money and no road map. What I did have was an authentic desire to find a better way. A few months later I went on a trailer food crawl with some girlfriends, but the trailers we wanted to visit were closed or we couldn't find them. Frustrated by this experience, I began connecting the dots of what would become the *Trailer Food Diaries*. I decided we needed a centralized resource with the inside scoop on the trailers. Namely, we needed to know where they were, what they were serving, and if they were any good. The lightbulb went on and I began blogging about a very interesting facet of the food industry that not only was in my heritage, but was blossoming in my hometown.

I became fascinated with all things trailer food. That fall, I partnered with a local production company to create the first-ever Gypsy Picnic Trailer Food Festival, which attracted thirty trailer food vendors and about twenty thousand Austinites. I began speaking publicly and entertaining in my home with trailer food recipes. I consulted with interested parties on how they could start trailer food parks in their areas.

Eating at the trailers is nostalgic, reminiscent of simpler times. Most of the chefs own their trailer operations and are the ones buying the supplies, cooking for you, ringing up your meal, sitting down with you to make sure you like it, and, of course, cleaning up after you leave. You get to behave more like you're at your crazy aunt's house than at a restaurant. The best part? You've gotten to eat some really good, reasonably priced food at your own pace.

In my research for this book, I have found some unique personalities who have contributed their best recipes, which I lovingly describe as eccentric, gourmet, home-cooked street food. With inspiration from my great-grandfather and the entrepreneurs I have met along the way, I have collected these recipes to share with you in your own pursuit of authenticity, and happiness.

Milton Harelik (Air Force), Sam Harelik (Navy), Louis Harelik (Army)

Haskell Harelik & Matley Paley Harelik

A Selective History of Austin

I speak a lot about my paternal great-grandfather as the immigrant-inspiration who turned his mobile food cart into an enterprise of five general stores. But it's the maternal side of my family that put down their roots in Austin, Texas. As a fourth-generation Austinite, I'm pretty sure Town Lake is in my blood. I did move out to Abilene during high school and spent periods of my life in other parts of the country, but I was born and raised in Austin. This is not your ordinary hometown, but it is a great place to be from and a great place to return.

Mimi, my centenarian grandmother Tura Hobbs, used to live on the corner of Red Bud Trail and Lake Austin Boulevard, close to the dam by Hula Hut. She will smile and tell you a story of a time when she would flirt with the trolley car driver so she wouldn't have to pay the nickel for him to take her down the street to Deep Eddy pool. The same pool where Pepa—Carl Hobbs—would later plant the big pecan trees that are still standing at both Deep Eddy and Barton Springs. The same pool where I learned how to swim. The same pool where I take my daughter today.

Pepa was postmaster here and was truly a great community leader—holding top posts in a long list of local and regional service organizations. He was a friend to all, from LBJ and Jake Pickle to the homeless who showed up at First Baptist Church. He also grew up farming four acres of spinach in Govalle—deep East Austin—picking it fresh and packing it in ice every morning during growing season, taking it to the farmers' market downtown, and also shipping it off on the railway express to markets in Chicago.

His own garden lined the perimeter of his backyard. I have sweet memories of picking mint for our tea, pulling carrots out of the ground, plucking ripe, juicy tomatoes (it broke his heart that I wouldn't eat them), eating jalapeño peppers and chewing ice the rest of the day, finding pecans to crack, shelling peas into brown paper bags, and getting muddy while helping move the water hose.

My mom and her two sisters were born and raised in Austin too, attending Austin, Reagan, and McCallum High Schools. Mom can tell you a story of a time when she rode in a jeep down the stairs of Mount Bonnell (not recommended for law-abiding citizens). She met my dad during their college years at the University of Texas at the Castilian dorm on 24th and San Antonio, interestingly the same corner where I would later live during college. If we ever stopped to count, we might find close to thirty other family members who attended "the University," including Pepa. Orange blood still runs through our veins and we look forward to getting together for nachos on football game days.

My folks were on campus in the late sixties, around the time that Austin became known as "the live music capital of the world." They witnessed local artists like Willie Nelson, Stevie Ray Vaughan, and Janis Joplin rising to the top of the scene as Austin gained national exposure. Speaking of music, that also runs in the family. My aunt played in the marching band at UT, and all of us girls took well to singing and playing piano, flute, and guitar. Some of us even did hand bells and sang in the church choir. We spent many a family get-together around the piano.

When I was growing up in Austin in the eighties, my dad owned Westlake Pharmacy on Bee Caves Road and my mom worked in the Capitol, at the Texas Senate. My mom took me to Whole Foods when it first opened on Lamar. I was three and loved getting strawberry smoothies and cheese quesadillas in the café before we shopped. I was involved in hunter/jumper horseback riding and volleyball. I swam three hundred days out of the year and loved my Labrador retriever. We went to Ballet Austin's *Nutcracker*, ate Mexican food, and went out for frozen yogurt. I did piano recitals at the Caswell House and had Girl Scout graduation ceremonies at the Zilker rose gardens. I climbed on our roof with my dad to watch the Fourth of July fireworks over the lake.

All the things I cherished about my childhood are things I still appreciate about Austin as an adult. I still walk Labradors (or "Labradogs," as my daughter calls them) around Lady Bird Lake, I still go wakeboarding on Lake Travis, I still eat nachos and wear orange on game day. I take my daughter to *The Nutcracker* every year, and we get smoothies at Whole Foods before we go shopping. I ride more bikes than I do horses these days, but I enjoy both. I have a garden, shop at the farmers' markets, take my one-hundred-year-old Mimi to get pedicures and wine, and volunteer with local civic organizations. Austin has a special place in my heart. I'm proud to be from here. It's a place, as my friend Roy Spence says, "where nobody is too good and everybody is good enough. It's a city of next, where if you can dream it, you can build it."

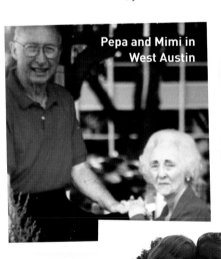

Pepa and Mimi in West Austin

Callie and Tiffany at Deep Eddy

Austin History Factoids

Austin's first name was Waterloo, back in the 1830s when it was just a village. Waterloo was the capital of the new Republic of Texas. Stephen F. Austin, the "Father of Texas," inherited an impresario grant from Spain from his father, Moses, that allowed him to bring three hundred families to colonize the area. Initially disinclined to follow his father's undertaking, Austin was persuaded by a letter from his mother, written only a few days before Moses died, and plans for colonization were set in motion. By 1825, the "Old Three Hundred" settled into more than sixty thousand acres in the Waterloo area. Austin was granted civil and military authority over the settlers and acquired contracts to bring nine hundred more families to the area. He established Freemasonry in the area and was elected to a leadership position in the new lodge.

War began with the Texas Revolution in 1835 with The Battle of Gonzales. After a series of battles, the Republic of Texas won independence from Mexico in 1836. Sam Houston, who had defeated General Santa Anna and the Mexican army at the last battle in San Jacinto, won the race for the first presidency of Texas. Austin served as the first secretary of state of the new republic for two months before he died from pneumonia. His last words were reported to be: "The independence of Texas is recognized! Don't you see it in the papers?"

In 1839, Republic of Texas President Mirabeau B. Lamar advised the Texas Congress to consider the Waterloo area as a capital location, noting that the pleasant surrounding hill country and its location on the river made it an opportune site between existing trade routes. The Waterloo location was chosen as the state capital and was given the name Austin. Edwin Waller laid out a fourteen-block grid on Congress Avenue between Shoal Creek and Waller Creek that would be the foundation of downtown Austin and the location for the Texas Capitol Building, which was completed in 1888. It remains the highest standing state capitol building in the United States.

A Day Trip to the Trailers: South Congress

It's the South Congress district that put Austin food trailers on the map. Live-music spots, hot rods, and off-the-wall boutiques serve as the backdrop for street fare that ranges from cupcakes to crepes to crunchy cones filled with chicken and special sauce. It's the perfect opportunity for casual al fresco dining, and don't worry if you can't decide what kind of food you want—SoCo has many offerings. Why not start with dessert at the south end of the strip? Hey Cupcake!—housed in a beautiful silver Airstream with a huge pink cupcake on top—gets credit for being the first trailer to set up shop on the 1600 block of South Congress. With multiple locations selling thousands of cupcakes every week, you can choose from delicacies including the "Michael Jackson," a chocolate cupcake with cream cheese topping, or the "Vanilla Dream," a vanilla cupcake with vanilla buttercream frosting.

Walking north from Hey Cupcake! toward downtown, you will hit a variety of trailer vendors. Many have come and gone over the last few years, but Mighty Cone has been a strong anchor at the far north end since March of 2009. The concept of the Mighty Cone—a variety of foods coated with the famous Hot 'n' Crunchy breading and served in paper cones—was developed by chef Jeff Blank of Hudson's on the Bend for the Austin City Limits Music Festival in 2002. Mighty Cone's offerings are classic trailer food: gourmet street fare that is both delicious and easy to walk around with. Try the Hot 'n' Crunchy Chicken Cone: breaded fried chicken topped with a mango-jalapeño slaw and ancho sauce, wrapped in a tortilla, and served in the signature cone.

As you're strolling through South Congress, be sure to plan time for nosing around some of the bohemian stores that keep Austin weird: Big Top Candy Shop, Lucy in Disguise with Diamonds, Crofts Original, Allens Boots, or Blackmail clothing boutique (located in the oldest commercial building on SoCo, which was originally a dry goods store in 1889). You can also make plans to stop in at local favorite Birds Barbershop for a cut, shave, or color. If you're hanging out on SoCo toward the evening, be sure to check out the lineup at the Continental Club, a legendary live music venue that has been stirring it up since the 1950s.

If you want to turn your day trip into something a little longer, you can spend the night at the Hotel San Jose, a bungalow-style hotel on South Congress, originally built in 1939. Another option is the Austin Motel, whose motto sums up a lot of the Austin spirit: "So close, yet so far out."

If you're on South Congress toward the beginning of the month, don't miss the district's monthly First Thursday event. During First Thursday, shops stay open late and additional street vendors set up outside as pedestrians stroll the sidewalks. It's a shopping/partying/eating/drinking experience that all ages can enjoy.

Breakfast

Migas à la Royito's

Courtesy of Royito's Hot Sauce Streamer

Royito's is all-natural, all-fresh Texas hot sauce with a mission statement—"Don't do mild"—to inspire people to up the spice, in life and in salsa. Enjoy this recipe as is, or add a tortilla to wrap it up and you've got yourself a hearty breakfast taco with heart. Yield: 2 servings.

4 large eggs
3 tablespoons olive oil
½ onion, finely chopped
½ bell pepper, finely chopped
2 tablespoons Royito's hot sauce
Handful of corn tortilla chips, crumbled
½ cup cheddar cheese, grated

- In a small bowl, lightly beat eggs and set aside.
- Heat oil in a heavy skillet, and sauté chopped onions and bell peppers for a couple of minutes.
- Stir in Royito's and crumbled tortilla chips and cook for 1 minute.
- Add the lightly beaten eggs and cook completely.
- Remove from heat and top with grated cheese.

Royito's

On the surface, you might think Roy Spence, with his history as the S of the illustrious GSD&M advertising agency, is an unusual suspect in the trailer food business, but his down-to-earth core values are the same as those of all the other vendors. In Roy's words, he is "working his way down the corporate ladder." He believes that America was "built on small," and he is passionate about supporting small local businesses. With his trailer, he believes he represents part of the larger movement to revitalize small business in America.

Although from an advertising standpoint he has represented such restaurants as Chili's, Romano's Macaroni Grill, On the Border, and many more corporate chains, Roy's experience with the food industry stops there and starts anew in his own kitchen. "I handmade tens of thousands of jars of hot sauce and sent them to restaurant owners and friends, and everyone kept asking, 'When can we buy this?' I finally decided I was cheating the world out of the opportunity to have a big dose of spice in their life," Roy says, with a big smile on his face. After fifteen years of experimentation, Roy came up with a unique and simple blend of fresh, natural ingredients that he combines to make Royito's hot sauce.

The hot sauce represents three of Roy's values that he learned from his father: be kind to everyone you meet, keep it simple, and don't do mild. In Roy's words, "The hot sauce is not a burning heat, but it's not mild. It's one flavor now, right where people like it." While the "Don't do mild" motto rings true in the taste of the hot sauce, the broader meaning is meant to inspire other entrepreneurs to not do anything mild in their endeavors and to truly live their dreams.

Upside-Down Apple and Smoked Bacon French Toast

Courtesy of Smokilicious Bar-B-Q

Although Smokilicious's owner used to gamble professionally, trying this version of Tony's French Toast is anything but risky. Serve this sweet and savory meal at a Sunday brunch, or to your sweetie in bed. Yield: 6–8 servings.

6 slices applewood-smoked bacon
5 eggs
¾ cup heavy cream (½ cup for egg mixture, ¼ cup to whip into caramelized sugar)
½ teaspoon ground cinnamon (¼ teaspoon for egg mixture, ¼ teaspoon for topping)
6 slices bread, sliced thick
½ stick butter, cubed
1 cup light brown sugar, plus ¼ teaspoon for topping
3 Granny Smith apples, peeled, cored, and cut into thin slices

- Preheat oven to 350°F.
- Cut bacon into small pieces. In a small skillet, cook, drain fat, and set aside.
- In a shallow dish, whisk eggs, ½ cup heavy cream, and ¼ teaspoon cinnamon until well combined. Lay the bread slices in the egg mixture and allow the liquid to be completely absorbed. Make sure both sides of the bread are completely coated.
- In a large, seasoned, cast-iron skillet over medium heat, add the butter and brown sugar and cook, stirring constantly, until sugar is caramelized.
- Remove from heat and gently whisk in the remaining ¼ cup heavy cream.
- Layer in the apple slices so there is a flat surface, and sprinkle bacon pieces on top.
- Next, arrange the soaked bread slices over the top so the apple slices are completely covered. You should be able to arrange the bread slices in a circular fan style, so there are no gaps. Or, if using a baking dish, lay flat side by side.
- Sprinkle the top with the remaining brown sugar and cinnamon and place pan on center rack in preheated oven. Bake for about 40 minutes, until the top is golden brown.
- Allow to cool for 5 minutes, then invert onto a large serving plate. Slice and serve.

Smokilicious Bar-B-Q

Former professional poker player Tony Alvarez started his Smokilicious Bar-B-Q trailer on a whim in February of 2010. In Tony's words, **"I've always had a passion for cooking, and being from Texas, I have a passion for BBQ. When I left Texas in 2003 for Reno, I was not finding the BBQ I was accustomed to and thought was the best. When I came back home to visit, I would get my fill of BBQ and good Tex-Mex food before heading back."** Tony comes by his culinary expertise honestly, having worked in kitchens and bars for about eighteen years both in private restaurants and at corporate chains. After noting that trailer-food culture was taking off, he decided that Austin was the perfect place to try his hand at perfecting his BBQ recipes before trying to launch his product and business. So he built a trailer and put all his passion into it.

The Smokilicious smoked brisket is his favorite item to cook and to eat. It's also his bestseller. Tony explains, "It's on our breakfast and lunch menu and outsells every item two to one. When I first started with the trailer, I was only going to do lunch, and I was getting there early to start smoking meat. People would come up and say, 'It smells good,' and ask if I had breakfast tacos." So Tony's breakfast menu was born. He started with the traditional bacon, egg, and cheese tacos but, understandably, people wanted brisket; it's hard to choose a traditional taco when you smell Tony's brisket.

A third-generation Austinite, Tony tries to buy everything as local as possible. If he has to buy from a grocer, he buys from City Market, an Austin-owned-and-operated grocery store. He buys Smoky Denmark sausage that is made here in town, and he purchases all of his slider rolls at Moonlight Bakery on South Lamar. Even his drinks are local: Hill Country water, Teas of Texas, and Ruta Maya coffee. Tony says, **"If I can get an item that is local that is what I'll use. We also try to recycle and do everything we can to be green."**

Bar-B-Q was always big in his family. He learned most of his cooking from his dad and uncles. **"From the very beginning I was interested in the cooking aspect. What it used to taste like is what I shoot for now. I know I got it right when it tastes like something I grew up with,"** Tony says. "I'm learning so much even though I've been doing it for a while. It's something I continue to learn. It's not like a job to me. I enjoy it, and I 'get' to do it." The trailer allows him to stay involved in the food industry while also giving him the flexibility to travel. Tony still travels back to Vegas and Reno to put on his poker face, but since business has picked up, he's playing more online and in Texas border towns.

Smoked Salmon and Cream Cheese Crepes

Courtesy of Flip Happy Crepes

Flip Happy was one of the original crepe food trailers in Austin, started by two friends. Gaining prominence with a Bobby Flay throwdown, this food is still considered gourmet home-cooking. Their motto is "Made from scratch with love." Yield: at least 6 crepes.

1½ cups whole milk
½ cup water
6 tablespoons butter, melted
3 large eggs
1½ cups all-purpose flour
¾ teaspoon salt
8 ounces cream cheese, softened
2 tablespoons lemon zest
1 medium shallot, minced
¼ cup capers, rinsed and chopped
1 tablespoon dill, minced
¼ teaspoon Asian fish sauce
Freshly ground pepper
Nonstick cooking spray
3 cups baby spinach (3 ounces)
1 teaspoon extra-virgin olive oil
1 teaspoon balsamic vinegar
½ pound smoked salmon, sliced
2 plum tomatoes, thinly sliced

1. In a bowl, whisk the milk with the water, melted butter, and eggs. Mix the flour and salt in another bowl. Whisk the milk mixture into the flour. Strain the batter into a measuring cup and refrigerate for 1 hour.

2. In a bowl, blend the cream cheese with the lemon zest, shallot, capers, dill, and fish sauce. Season with pepper.

3. Spray a 12-inch nonstick skillet with cooking spray. Heat the skillet over moderate heat. Pour ⅓ cup of the batter into the skillet and swirl the pan to coat it evenly. Cook the crepe until light gold on the bottom, about 1 minute. Flip and cook for about 30 seconds longer. Transfer to a plate and repeat with the remaining batter.

4. In a bowl, toss the spinach with the oil and vinegar.

5. Fold each crepe in half. Spread 2 tablespoons of cream cheese vertically down the center of each crepe and lay a couple of salmon slices over it. Top with spinach and tomatoes and season with pepper. Fold one side of the crepe over the filling, roll to close (like a burrito), and serve.

Flip Happy Crepes

Nessa grew up in the Caribbean
and moved to Austin in the nineties
by way of the Midwest and New
Orleans. Andrea also spent some
time living in New Orleans, but she
originally comes from Houston.
After meeting her husband, Patrick
Gannon, in New York, he took her to
Ireland, his homeland, and she fell
in love with him and the crepes she
tried there. Since no one was doing
crepes out of an Airstream in Austin
in 2006, the dynamic duo decided
to put their plan into action and
manifest their food trailer business
crepe-style. While Nessa favors the
fried egg and ham with gruyere and
mornay sauce and Andrea prefers
the spinach feta with garlic aioli,
their fan favorite is the Cuban and
pork crepes, which happened to
beat Bobby Flay in a Food Network
Throwdown.

Rockefeller Quiche with Tasso Hollandaise

Courtesy of Kate's Southern Comfort

This dish makes a decadent meal anytime, as it can be served for breakfast/brunch or as an appetizer or light supper. It's easy to make, using some shortcuts, and the sauce can be put on anything. Serve with fruit or a side salad and mimosas or Bloodies! If making appetizers, simply use miniature tart/muffin pans. Yield: 3–4 servings.

Crust:
2 cups instant grits

- Cook grits according to package directions until very thick. Chill.
- Pat into an even, ¼-inch thick layer in a pie plate, forming a pie crust.

Rockefeller Quiche:
1 box frozen spinach
1 cup onion, diced
3 cloves garlic, minced
2 ribs celery, chopped finely
¾ cup melted butter
3 tablespoons parsley, chopped
1½ teaspoons sea salt
½ teaspoon cayenne
2 teaspoons lemon pepper
½ to 1 cup grated Parmesan
6 eggs, beaten untill fluffy
1 cup heavy cream

- Preheat oven to 350°F.
- Defrost spinach and drain well.
- Sauté onion, garlic, and celery in butter until golden.
- Cool slightly and mix in remaining ingredients.
- Pour into crust and bake until inserted toothpick comes out clean, about 1 hour.

Tasso Hollandaise:
2 cups hollandaise sauce (can be from a mix but better from scratch)
1 cup tasso (or andouille sausage), browned and diced

Make hollandaise according to instructions and add meat.

Kate's Southern Comfort

The concept behind Kate's Southern Comfort is Louisiana fried pies. The pies are "affordable for me to make, affordable for anyone to eat, and they are good grab-and-go food that you can take on a picnic, down to (Barton) Springs, or eat at the trailer," Kate says. She grew up in East Texas in the early '60s eating some pretty bland casseroles, but upon moving to Louisiana, Kate learned to cook from people's grandmothers at big Sunday-afternoon family get-togethers.

Kate's fried pies involve an Argentine crust, and she makes all the fillings from scratch. The Nak.i.tish has a spicy, peppery pork filling that is super savory. Although her crusts do contain some beef fat, she gives a nod to her vegetarian customers with the Humble Pie, which involves mustard, collard greens, and sweet potato. Diners might also be interested in the Bleudan, which was made by mistake but contains boudin sausage and bleu cheese. Although Kate claims not to have a bestseller or a personal favorite, she speaks highly of the current special, a hatch green chile, chicken, and cheese fried pie that melts in your mouth. But don't take Kate's word for it: she's had customers from New Orleans who have been so impressed that they had to call their meemaw and come back for a second helping.

Porkey's Donut

Courtesy of Gourdough's

"Big. Fat. Donuts" is what the side of the Gourdough's Airstream reads—and with the Porkey's, a big fat donut is what you'll get. Canadian bacon, whipped cream cheese, and jalapeño jelly top off a fresh donut. Mama didn't raise no fool!

Donut(s) (this is not Gourdough's donut but a good substitute for home use):
¼ to ½ teaspoon active dry yeast
1½ cups warm water (110°F/45°C)
½ cup white sugar
1 teaspoon salt
2 eggs
1 cup evaporated milk
7 cups all-purpose flour, divided
¼ cup shortening
1 quart vegetable oil for frying

1. In a large bowl, dissolve yeast in warm water. Add sugar, salt, eggs, and evaporated milk and blend well. Mix in 4 cups of the flour and beat until smooth. Add the shortening, and then the remaining 3 cups of flour. Cover and chill for up to 24 hours (3 hours will work if you're in a hurry).

2. Roll out dough 1-inch thick. Use the top of a drinking glass to cut donut circles and use a butter knife to cut out holes in the middle. Fry in 350°F hot oil for about 5 minutes, turning frequently. If donuts do not pop up, oil is not hot enough. Drain on paper towels. (Makes at least 2 dozen donuts.)

Jalapeño Jelly:
¾ pound jalapeño peppers
2 cups cider vinegar, divided
6 cups sugar
3 (3-ounce) envelopes liquid pectin

1. After removing stems and seeds from jalapeños, puree in food processor with 1 cup cider vinegar.

2. Combine puree, additional 1 cup cider vinegar, and sugar in large sauce pot. Bring to a boil; boil for 10 minutes, stirring constantly.

3. Stir in liquid pectin. Return to a rolling boil and boil hard for 1 minute, stirring constantly.

4. Remove from heat. Skim foam if necessary.

5. Follow standard canning procedures. For a milder version of the recipe, substitute bell peppers for jalapeño peppers.

Canadian Bacon:
Brown Canadian bacon in some butter in a sauté pan. Cut into 1- to 2-inch strips.

Now you're ready to start building...
1. Fill the donut with jalapeño jelly in 5 to 6 places. The best way to fill the donut with jelly at home is by using an injector for seasoning turkey. Flip donut over, and fill donut hole with jelly also.

2. Spread whipped cream cheese on donut and top it off with pieces of the Canadian bacon.

Gourdough's

Gourdough's owners and real estate company partners Ryan Palmer and Paula Samford got their first taste of the food industry when they opened their donut trailer for business during the Austin City Limits Music Festival in October of 2009. So how did these two stumble into their popular oversized-donut business? In Ryan's words, **"It was kind of by luck. We worked long weekends and showed property all day without eating, and we'd be starving. Paula's mom and grandmom used to make her donuts that were simple, with cinnamon and sugar. We would make those as an indulgent thing at the house. We started making them for friends, and they started suggesting different ideas, and before we knew it we had a notebook full of ideas."**

With over twenty delectable oversized options to choose from out of the thirty-foot, '78 Sovereign Airstream trailer, it's as hard to make a selection as it is to finish one. Porky's is Ryan's favorite. He also suggests the Funky Monkey, which was inspired by his memories of New Orleans, where he lived for five years. The Funky Monkey is based on the bananas foster concept but on a donut: cream cheese icing and grilled bananas with brown sugar. The Flying Pig is their bestseller. It's the one with bacon and maple syrup icing.

And in case you didn't catch the play on words, the company name is meant to signify "gourmet dough" while also using the Spanish word *gordo,* which means "fat." Fat you will get if you make Gourdough's a regular stop, but don't let the calories scare you; the calories in Gourdough's donuts are reduced by half when eaten with a friend.

Lucky J's Waffle Breakfast Tacos

Courtesy of Lucky J's Chicken & Waffles

"Chicken for strength, waffles for speed" is the tagline on Jason Umlas's food trailer. However, after eating this version of breakfast tacos, you'll be ready for a nap. Yield: 4 servings.

Waffle Mix:
1 cup flour
1 teaspoon sugar
¾ teaspoon baking powder
½ teaspoon salt
2 tablespoons vegetable oil
¾ cup water
½ cup buttermilk
1 egg

Combine ingredients, and allow batter to sit for 15 minutes before using. Ladle approximately 5 ounces of batter into a hot, well-seasoned, standard 7-inch waffle iron (not a Belgian waffle iron). Cook for 2–3 minutes until golden in color.

Breakfast Potatoes:
¼ cup vegetable oil
1 cup red potatoes, ¾-inch dice
½ cup red onions, ¾-inch dice
1 teaspoon seasoning salt
½ teaspoon dried rosemary
½ teaspoon dried thyme

Heat oil to medium high and add potatoes and onions. Sauté until the potatoes are crispy. Drain any excess oil, then toss with the seasonings.

Waffle Breakfast Tacos:
1 cup breakfast potatoes
4 slices cooked bacon, cut into 1-inch pieces
4 eggs
4 slices cheddar cheese
4 waffles
Shredded cheese

Combine breakfast potatoes and bacon on a hot flattop or in a nonstick sauté pan over a medium-high flame. Allow the contents of the pan to heat through thoroughly (about 1 to 2 minutes). Add the eggs to the pan and stir occasionally so that the eggs "scramble" slightly. In the meantime, place a slice of cheddar cheese on each waffle. When the eggs are thoroughly cooked (about 4 minutes or until there are no runny parts visible), divide scramble into four parts and place in the center of each waffle. Top with shredded cheese; fold the waffles and serve.

Lucky J's Chicken & Waffles

Don't let the charming quirkiness of Jason Umlas's food trailer fool you; the chicken and waffle concept was a deliberate business model highlighting a profitable breakfast-food menu along with the niche market of real Southern fried chicken. But Lucky J's is more than a place to bring the hipster palette. Jason's spot over on the East Side hosts DJs and live gospel music along with some pretty spectacular campfires. He's not from here, but he sure fits in well. Why Austin? **"Being from New York and then LA I'm accustomed to having a diverse group of people. For Austin being a smaller city, it's great in that regard. You can have grandparents wearing tie-dye sitting by punk teenagers sitting by a family of four, all enjoying chicken and waffles around a campfire and getting along."**

Jason describes the Ms. M's waffle taco as one of the fan favorites. It's a handheld wrap that includes boneless fried chicken strips with bacon and Swiss plus a little powdered sugar. Wait, what? And if you need help starting your own trailer vendor business, check out Jason's consulting firm: Lucky U's. Get it? For new vendors, Jason reminds you that your ego is not always your amigo. If your business plan doesn't make sense on paper, it's not going to make cents on the street. Lucky for you, Lucky U's is there to help you launch your business strategy.

Zeppole

Courtesy of Osmo's Kitchen

Zeppole are tasty Italian-American donuts that taste great with a rich coffee or espresso for breakfast. Yield: 10–12 servings.

2 cups flour
1 envelope of active dry yeast
1 cup warm water
1 tablespoon sugar
1 teaspoon kosher salt
2 tablespoon unsalted butter, softened
Canola or vegetable oil for frying
Confectioner's sugar for sprinkling

- Sift the flour into a bowl and set aside.
- Dissolve the yeast in the warm water (110–115°F) until it blooms. It will look milky, and takes about 5 to 8 minutes.
- Add the sugar to the yeast and, with a dough hook attachment, mix while adding the flour and salt.
- When the dough starts to come together, add the butter and incorporate until the dough forms a ball.
- Remove the dough and place in a lightly oiled bowl. Place the bowl in a warm spot in your kitchen and cover lightly with plastic wrap. Let it rise for about an hour and a half.
- Heat oil to 375°F and drop the zeppole by rounded tablespoons into the hot oil. With a wire net, turn them over until golden brown. Set on paper towels and generously sift the confectioner's sugar on top.

Osmo's Kitchen

Kent and Robin O'Keefe each had over twenty years of cooking experience when they met at the Culinary Institute of America in New York. Prior to starting their food trailer, they owned a catering company in Austin called Two Bodacious Chefs. **They chose Austin because they both felt at home here. Their Osmo's Kitchen trailer developed out of their love of culinary arts and offers a combination of Italian and Cajun cuisine.**

When you walk up to the trailer with unique paintings on its side, you'll probably hear zydeco music coming from inside or maybe Stevie Ray Vaughn, Ray Charles, The Allman brothers, Led Zeppelin, or ZZ Top. If you ask Kent, his wife's Sicilian gravy with meatballs and pasta takes the cake, but their bestseller happens to be the blackened catfish po' boy with spicy slaw. He says the best part about the business, besides the actual cooking, is interacting with the customers and seeing people enjoy what he and Robin have prepared.

Muffins

Courtesy of Little Bean Bakery & Café

The chef's personal favorite recipe. Add the fruit, nut, or chocolate chip of your choice. The topping is at the baker's discretion, but remember, too much of a good thing is too much for your muffin. Yield: 12 muffins or 24 cupcakes.

½ pound salted butter
2 cups sour cream
2 cups sugar
3 eggs
2 teaspoon vanilla
3 cups sifted flour
3 teaspoons baking powder
1½ teaspoons baking soda
Any topping: fruit, nuts, chocolate chips, etc.

- Preheat oven to 375°F and prep muffin tins.
- Melt butter, bring to room temperature, and add it to a bowl with the sour cream while beating on low.
- Add sugar and beat on low until mixed, then add eggs and vanilla and mix until blended well.
- Combine dry ingredients in separate bowl. Add dry ingredients to the wet mixture and blend well.
- Mix in your treat of choice and spoon batter into the muffin cups.
- Bake for 20 to 25 minutes.

Little Bean Bakery & Café

The Little Bean Bakery & Café started as an idea for a bake sale for Share Our Strength, a national nonprofit working to end childhood hunger. After preliminary research, Michelle Glenn decided she could make an even bigger impact by opening a food trailer and donating a portion of her profits to the effort. Hence, the Little Bean trailer opened in March of 2011.

Her favorite thing on the menu is the muffins, the result of her and her mom experimenting with an old coffee cake recipe. But the cookies are her true inspiration for baking. **Her mother used to have cookie-baking parties for all the kids in the neighborhood, and Michelle has precious memories of the messes and milk and cookies from her youth.** Speaking of youth, "little bean," is a nickname for her daughter and another inspiration behind the trailer.

Beignets

Courtesy of Little Bean Bakery & Café

Grab a cup of joe and sit down with the newspaper. Austin isn't New Orleans, but sometimes we like to pretend. Yield: 12 servings of 4.

2¼ teaspoons active dry yeast
1½ cups water
½ cup sugar
1 teaspoon salt
2 eggs
1 cup evaporated milk
7 cups flour (divided), sifted
¼ cup shortening
2 teaspoons almond extract
  (cinnamon extract is tasty too)
1 quart vegetable oil for frying
Honey
Powdered sugar

- In large bowl, dissolve yeast in warm water. Add sugar, salt, eggs, extract, and evaporated milk and blend. Add 4 cups of flour and mix until smooth. Add the shortening and the remaining 3 cups of flour and mix to incorporate. Make sure not to overwork your dough!
- Divide the dough into baseball-sized balls and roll out to about ¼-inch thin circles. Cut each circle into quarters.
- Heat oil between 350° and 375°, no more, no less. Fry to a golden brown. If the dough does not puff out, then the oil is not hot enough.
- Drizzle with honey and cover with powdered sugar.

COLD BREW e.com
elixercoffee.com
HIGH OCTANE SIX 30z SWIGS

elixer

COLD BREW

ICED COFFEE
"JUST BLACK"
COLD BREWED - LOW ACID
CAFFEINATED - NO SUGAR

Drinks

Homemade Basil Lemonade

Courtesy of That's Amore

If you're hankering for some bona fide home-cooked Italian food, Angela will be pleased to serve you paninis, salads, cannolis, and more out of her vintage Airstream. This homemade basil lemonade is a refreshing elixir to revive your energy and attitude. Yield: 4–6 servings.

2 cups basil simple syrup (see below)
2 cups fresh-squeezed lemon juice
2 cups cold San Pellegrino sparkling water

To make simple syrup:
1 cup water
1 bunch fresh basil
2 cups sugar

- Cooking on stove top, bring water to a boil and add basil and sugar; stir until sugar dissolves.
- Place in a bowl on an ice bath. Run liquid through strainer when cooled.

To make lemonade:
Mix simple syrup into remaining ingredients. Serve over ice.

That's Amore

Hunkered down in the South Shore Eatery on East Riverside, Angela Melia's Italian-themed '74 Airstream features paninis, salads, soups, and cannolis, which can all be made to order. With twenty years' experience as a chef and in restaurant management, and with a spitfire personality and a keen interest in doing things right, the business is evidently in her blood.

Eating at That's Amore feels like being at an Italian family home for dinner. The menu was inspired by Angela's Sicilian grandparents, all of whom have an item named after them. Each panini is memorable for its flavor and heart. The Sicilian mixes Italian sausage with bell peppers, fennel, and mozzarella. The House Salad includes a romaine and spring mix with celery, tomatoes, hearts of palm, cucumber, and pepperoncini-, kalamata-, and green pimento–stuffed olives. The Cherry Pistachio Cannoli is just one of her dessert delicacies.

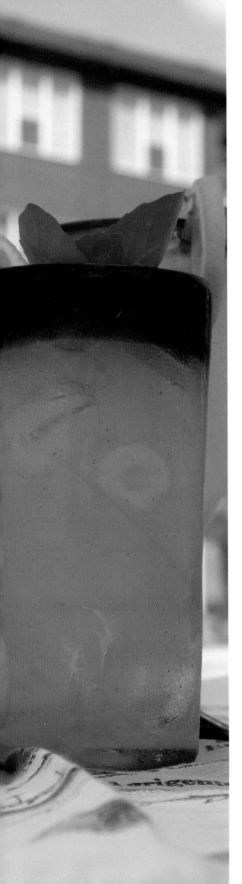

The Double Barrel

Courtesy of Gonzo Juice

Aptly named, this intense juice is like a shotgun. Pow!

In a blender, combine these fresh-squeezed juices:

5 ounces carrot juice
1½ ounces grapefruit juice
½ ounce lemon juice
Ginger juice to taste
Garlic juice to taste
Jalapeño juice to taste

Warning: This recipe contains a strong garlic portion, so adjust to taste. You will smell garlicky.

Gonzo Juice

Brother and sister partners Sutton and Bella spent their early years in New Mexico and then toured the country in a school bus. They have firsthand experience putting a sliding pot back on the stove while a bus is in motion. Though both tried their hand in the corporate world, they independently decided it wasn't for them. As a result, the Gonzo Juice concept was initiated just forty days after Sutton purchased the trailer.

"Gonzo" is a nod to Hunter S. Thompson's Gonzo journalism style as well as the pimp Muppet from space who always had a harem of chickens at his side. Gonzo ultimately married one of the chickens, Camilla, another nickname for the trailer, which boasts a large rooster head in its architecture.

For lunch, the Saddlebag Salad is most popular. It can also be made as a wrap and utilizes the following taco salad–esque ingredients: romaine lettuce, Fritos, carrots, corn, black beans, cotija cheese, avocado, ranch, and hot sauce. The Melon Patch is the bestselling juice and contains watermelon, orange, and lemon juice.

Single-Cup Pour-Over Coffee

Courtesy of Patika Coffee

Patika is a Turkish word that means "footpath" but also implies a hidden pathway. Back in the 1500s, some of the first coffeehouses in the world opened in Istanbul, and they were outlawed for their popularity. For this reason, many of them would set up in back alleys and footpaths, forming the original speakeasies. Since Andy and Nick of Patika Coffee were inspired by the concept of a coffeehouse off the beaten path, and since they are on a well-traveled beat downtown, the name Patika was a perfect fit for their otherworldly coffee and refreshing teas.

Pour-Over:

Fresh coffee is good. Stale coffee is bad. To make the freshest coffee possible, Patika offers pour-over coffee handmade to order. To make your own at home, it's best to start with freshly roasted (within a week or so) whole-bean coffee.

Ideally you'll use about 21 grams (about 3 tablespoons) of ground coffee for 12 ounces of water.

You'll also need:
- A good grinder (preferably a burr grinder, which gives a more consistent grind size)
- A pour-over filter holder
- Filters (there is a wide variety, including paper, Swissgold, and cloth, and there are arguments to be made for each one)
- Hot water kettle

1. Starting with clear, filtered water (but not distilled), bring the kettle to a boil. As it's heating up, grind your coffee. You'll want grounds that are soft, but still a touch gritty. It should form into a clump when you press it between your thumb and forefinger.

2. Empty the coffee into your filter. Depending on the type of filter you use, you may want to rinse it before you put the coffee in, as some filters can leave a papery taste in the coffee. It's best to taste a batch of coffee and see if you notice a paper taste. If so, rinse the filter first by pouring some hot water through it.

3. Water boils at 212°F, and you really want your water to be around 195°. So let it cool down for 30 to 40 seconds. Or, if you have a gooseneck kettle, you can pour the boiled water into the kettle, wait 10 to 20 seconds, and the water will cool to the temperature you're looking for.

4. Pour a bit of the water over the grounds, just enough to wet the grounds and let them absorb the water and swell. This should take about 20 to 30 seconds.

5. After the grounds have become saturated and look a little "dry" again (resembling the top of a muffin), begin to pour very slowly into the center of the grounds. The rate you pour at should be similar to the rate of the coffee coming out the bottom of the filter holder. Continue pouring until you have a delicious, fresh cup of coffee. The pour should ideally take about 3 minutes to extract the coffee properly.

Patika

Andy Wigginton and Nick Krupa kicked their software careers to pursue happiness via coffee. Their inspiration for Patika came five years prior to opening, when they were on vacation in San Francisco. "We came across a coffee cart [Blue Bottle] at the farmers' market that had a huge swarm of people around it. We had the best lattes we'd ever had. Their original location was a tucked-away garage door in Hayes Valley. We make it a ritual to visit every time we go back, and we now have a quest to find really great coffee in great cities."

The partners say that Austin is a great place to start a high-end coffee business. In their words, "The community is really supportive of small businesses; everyone is very laid back and has a very open and accepting attitude where if you want to try something different in a different way, they like that and embrace it. We have a great lifestyle. Anyone who comes here feels it. Being downtown, we meet a lot of tourists, and they talk about how Austin feels like a nice place where people are appreciative of the outdoors and nice people. Having lived in California, New York, and Europe, Austin feels like the right combination of a lot of stuff to do within a rather small community—although we could turn the temperature down about fifteen degrees."

Elixer Iced Coffee —The Home Version

Courtesy of Elixer Coffee

It's hard to resist coffee from a '52 Studebaker whose converted flatbed contains an espresso machine.

We suggest using a French press with coarsely ground coffee beans, with a 1:4 ratio of one part beans and four parts water. Fill French press the night before and add a pinch of cardamom powder from one cardamom seed, a tiny pinch of nutmeg, and a dash of cinnamon. Let steep overnight, press in the morning, and you'll have the best cup of iced coffee, Elixer style. Just remember to use room-temperature water and to leave the press on the counter overnight.

Elixer Coffee

A former pediatric nurse, Keturah Somerville wanted to spend more time with her kids, so she decided to open a coffee shop. On Craigslist, in Tuscon, Arizona, she found a '52 Studebaker with a converted flatbed that was already outfitted with an espresso machine, and she was ready to roll.

Keturah loves talking with her customers and getting to know them. Many of the older customers enjoy sharing Studebaker-related stories from their youth. One retired couple stops by regularly to chat and hula hoop with Keturah.

"I have three children and two of them have been avid coffee drinkers since they were very little. I'm sure they'll be able to grow up and tell stories about the disk that comes out of the espresso maker. When you pull a shot, you have a little 2-inch by 1-inch puck—my babies love to break them into crumbles in the yard—they get covered in grounds and reek of coffee for days."

Café con Leche

Courtesy of The Texas Cuban

Hector Ward is the real "Texas Cuban," and his recipes are inspired by traditional family recipes. Yield: 3–5 servings.

10 tablespoons sugar
2 ½ cups milk
3 cups Café Bustelo instant espresso

- Pour sugar into a small pot on low heat and begin to caramelize. Stop heating sugar when it has turned into a liquid (light brown) caramel substance.
- In a separate pan, heat milk to a low simmer, then pour into the caramelized sugar.
- Add Café Bustelo. Stir the mixture well and serve.

The Texas Cuban

Hector Ward is the real "Texas Cuban." He grew up in southwest Houston on a cattle ranch that has been in his family for 120 years. He is the first born of a Cuban refugee. His parents came over to the United States via boat when Castro came into power when they were both only thirteen years old. Many other family members followed, landing in Miami. In fact, a lot of the recipes from the Texas Cuban trailer are inspired by traditional family recipes from Hector's grandmother, aunts, and mother.

As to be expected, the Texas Cuban sandwich is one of the trailer's bestsellers. Other favorites include the croquettes, which involve mango nectar shipped from Egypt to Miami to Austin, and the Media Noche sandwich. The Papa Rellena offers a scrumptious take on hamburger meat, which is cooked with green bell peppers and olives, balled up and surrounded with mashed potatoes, and deep-fried in the healthiest possible of oils. Have a Mexican coke with real sugar and some plantain chips with The Papa, and you'll be set.

Hector cooked throughout his younger years in the commercial-food industry and in the family kitchen before becoming a musician. During the economic downturn of 2009, he and some of his band members decided to pool resources and try their hand at the trailer food business. Hector Ward and the Big Time is Hector's ten-piece band, and he employs not only his own band members at The Texas Cuban but other musicians as well. "We're all certified to do what we do in the kitchen. It's just a way to get the good food out there and put good people to work," Hector reports.

The Cake Shake

Courtesy of Holy Cacao

Yes, it's hard to believe something so deliciously indulgent can be so easy, but to make a Cake Shake all you need is milk, ice cream, and cake! Although the flavor combo possibilities are endless, red velvet cake with vanilla ice cream is hands down Holy Cacao's bestseller. They bake from scratch, but Betty Crocker will work too.

¾ cup whole milk
2 scoops ice cream (we prefer Blue Bell)
Approximately 3 chunks of cake that measure 4 inches by 2 inches
Whipped cream

- Add milk to blender first, then ice cream, and finally cake.
- Blend well for half a minute.
- Pour into a glass, garnish with whipped cream, and enjoy!

Holy Cacao

After dating for three months, Ellen and John decided to go into the cake ball business together. Thus, Holly the Holy Cacao Cow was born on South First on March 23, 2009. When they were developing their concept, Ellen really liked the idea of focusing on hot chocolate, taking inspiration from her positive experiences in New York. Understandably, John had his concerns about hot chocolate in, well, Austin. But Ellen's entrepreneurial spirit prevailed. "Ben & Jerry's makes ice cream in Vermont," she argued. Red Velvet Cake Balls are the bestseller, but if you want to try John's personal favorite go for the Brass Peanut Butter, which has yummalicious crunched-up Nutter Butters inside.

Holy Cacao Hot Chocolate

Courtesy of Holy Cacao

For another easy but decadent dessert experience, simply use equal parts milk, cream, and chocolate for hot chocolate the way it was meant to be.

1 cup whole milk
1 cup heavy whipping cream
Dash of Madagascar bourbon
  vanilla (optional)
1 cup bittersweet chocolate
  chips

- Stir milk, cream, and a dash of vanilla into pan and warm over low heat for 5 minutes.
- Turn heat to medium and add chocolate.
- Whisk constantly for a couple of minutes, or until the chocolate has melted completely.
- Pour and enjoy!

Blueberry Smoothie

Courtesy of Bufalo Bob's Chalupa Wagon

A blueberry smoothie a day keeps the doctor away.

½ cup low-fat yogurt
½ cup blueberries
¼ cup applesauce
¼ cup orange juice
1 tablespoon honey

- Put ingredients into a blender and mix for about 1 minute.
- Pour into a 12-ounce cup and serve.

Bufalo Bob's

With a focus on healthy local products, Bufalo Bob uses only range-fed bison and chicken, locally produced, without hormones or antibiotics. His chicken comes from Buddy's Natural Chicken in Gonzales, Texas, and the bison hails from the Madroño Ranch just outside of Kerrville.

Bufalo Bob takes traditional Mexican street food to new heights in creative cuisine, using the chalupa as a palette and offering toppings such as ceviche, hummus, flaxseed meal, chopped green olives, ground bison, marinated artichoke hearts, roasted red peppers, and other yummy ingredients.

A Day Trip to the Trailers: East Austin

Nestled in Austin's artistic and still-developing East Side, the East 6th Street trailer community is bustling with chicken and waffles, Vietnamese sandwiches, kombucha, baked goods, hot dogs, pizza, cheesesteak sandwiches, and knock-yer-socks-off coffee. All this and more can be found just across the highway from the popular expanse of 6th Street, known for its bar and live-music scene. The east side of Austin is also home to local favorite Boggy Creek Farm, an organic urban market farm that supplies many of these trailers with their garden-grown goodies.

The two main trailer parks on East 6th are separated by only a few blocks and are within easy walking or biking distance of each other. East Side Drive-In isn't hard to spot: just look for the big red double-decker #19 bus serving Philly cheesesteaks and playing loud music. At any given time, there are six to eight trailers open for business at East Side Drive-In. Once you've had your fill, you can stroll down to the other East 6th trailer park at 6th and Waller. This park has a little more breathing room than East Side Drive-In and some shade trees, and boasts an equal variety of trailer-food vendors, including Lucky J's Chicken & Waffles, Spartan Pizza, and the Asian-fusion truck, Me So Hungry.

When visiting either of these parks, remember that trailers are, of course, mobile and subject to location changes. And while you're on the East Side, be sure to take time to visit the artist studios and some of the best bars: East Side Show Room, Shangri-La, Rio Rita, East End Wines, Uncorked, The Grackle, and The Liberty (the last two of which boast food trailer East Side King out front and back, respectively).

Appetizers, Snacks, Lagniappes, and other little tidbits

Watermelon and Goat Cheese Wedge Salad

Courtesy of Luke's Inside Out

Gourmet watermelon ideas meet . . . Pop Rocks. Brilliant. Check it out.

Watermelon triangle wedges
  with rinds intact
Goat cheese
Pop Rocks
Sunflower sprouts
Rosemary

Use triangle-shaped wedge of watermelon as a base and top with goat cheese, Pop Rocks, sunflower sprouts, and rosemary.

Luke's Inside Out

Luke Bibby is the chef behind Luke's Inside Out. After catering private parties and running concession stands at music festivals in Austin for fifteen years, popular demand led him to open up a food trailer. He prides himself on specializing in "out there" cuisine, which is anything he happens to be cooking at the time with some uniquely Luke final touches. For example, he whipped up a Korean Rabbit with Tater Tots Sandwich that was a fan favorite. His atypical watermelon salad combines sweet with savory and sour to create a gustatory experience that will keep your taste buds guessing. Try any of his "Traioli" sauces to add some extra flavor to your sandwich. Specifically, you might go with the love sauce. Don't be shy. If you want to know how to make love sauce, Luke makes love twice a day and is willing to teach you, too.

His trailer is currently hitched up to the Gibson bar in South Austin just off South Lamar, where you can catch him for lunch and dinner every day. If you hit him up for a special catering event, you'll join the list of accomplished musicians he has served, including ZZ Top, Crosby, Stills and Nash, Beck, the Allman Brothers, Asleep at the Wheel, Lyle Lovett, Tool, Joan Baez, Outkast, Snoop Dog, Steve Earl, and more.

African Peanut Soup (Mafe)

Courtesy of Cazamance

Mafe (pronounced ma-fay) is as popular and familial in West Africa as mashed potatoes are in the States. Just as you might find Creole-influenced mashed potatoes in New Orleans and Italian-spiced mashed potatoes in New York, Mafe has multiple variations depending on the traditions of different regions. This is Chef Iba's version. Yield: 4 servings.

1 sweet yellow onion, diced
2 carrots, diced
1 large sweet potato, peeled and diced
2 medium potatoes, diced
1 15-ounce can chickpeas
1 zucchini
1 squash

2 cloves garlic
1 soupspoon paprika
3 sprigs thyme
Salt to taste
Pepper to taste
1 soupspoon peanut butter (creamy or chunky)
Cayenne pepper to taste
White basmati rice, cooked

1. Place onion, carrots, and sweet potato in a saucepan and cover with water. Bring to a boil, then reduce heat and simmer until tender (about 15 to 20 minutes). Stir occasionally to prevent sticking.

2. In a large soup pot, place potatoes, chickpeas, zucchini, and squash, and cover with water. Bring to a boil, then reduce heat and simmer until tender (about 45 minutes). Some of the vegetables will dissolve in the soup, and some will stay in chunks.

3. Add garlic, paprika, thyme, salt, pepper, and pan full of onion, carrots, and sweet potato. Boil again (another 5 minutes).

4. Add peanut butter to the soup pot, stir to dissolve, and boil for 5 more minutes. Keep the lid closed and cook on high heat. Add additional peanut butter and cayenne to taste.

5. Serve soup over rice as a main dish, or serve independently as an appetizer or light meal.

Cazamance

Iba is a self-taught foodie from South Africa who well understands the phrase "the eyes eat first." Although his menu is African-inspired, Iba draws on many flavors from various cultures to offer a cuisine that is uniquely his. The Bunny Chow is a favorite among customers and can best be described as a hollowed piece of bread stuffed with a heavenly concoction of meat and spices. Iba says this dish was created during Apartheid, when poor blacks working in kitchens would hide meat in bread to give to their families.

Eating at Cazamance gives you the full trailer experience of community, good food, and a friendly Austin vibe under the shade trees. It's across the street from Clive Bar, and smack downtown off Red River and Cesar Chavez. If you're grabbing a drink at Clive, Iba will walk an order over to you so you can eat at your barstool.

Roasted Tomato and Vegetable Soup

Courtesy of All-City Subs

All-City Subs provides a *Sopranos*-esque experience with locally sourced, hot-roasted Italian-style sandwiches and soups.

10 to 12 tomatoes of different varieties, or whatever you have
½ sweet yellow onion, cut into large chunks
6 to 7 garlic cloves, with skins on
1 tablespoon olive oil
Sea salt to taste
Freshly cracked pepper to taste
4 cups vegetable broth
3 carrots, diced
2 celery stalks, diced
1 zucchini, diced
2 cups kale, chopped
1 (15-ounce) can garbanzo beans or white beans, drained and rinsed
6 to 7 fresh basil leaves, finely shredded

- Preheat oven to 375°F. Line a baking sheet with tin foil, then coat with cooking spray.
- Quarter the tomatoes, cut the onions, and separate the garlic cloves (keep skins on so they don't burn). Spread the tomatoes, onions, and garlic over the lined baking sheet. Drizzle with olive oil, then sprinkle with sea salt and pepper; toss to coat.
- Place in the oven and roast for 30 to 40 minutes, or until the onions and garlic are very soft and the tomatoes are still juicy.
- Remove from the oven and let cool. Once cooled, carefully peel the skins off the cloves of garlic. Spoon the tomatoes, onions, garlic, and juices into a small Dutch oven, then add the vegetable broth. Using an immersion blender, blend the vegetables until smooth, making sure there are no chunks.
- Add the carrots and celery; cook for 30 minutes or until vegetables are tender. Add the zucchini, kale, and garbanzo beans and cook for 5 more minutes.

All-City Subs

Drummer J. K. Bellucci played in Austin several times while on tour before moving here and opening All-City Subs. Drawing from family recipes and twenty years of experience working in practically every facet of the service industry, he put together an all-star menu that features some of his favorite sandwiches.

Based loosely on a recipe from The Mix, a restaurant in Philadelphia, J. K.'s pork sandwich is hugely popular. He brushes garlic-infused canola oil onto a sweet Italian roll and toasts it, then builds the sandwich with homemade mustard, collard greens, slow-roasted pork dipped in *au jus*, sweet pickled onions, and smoked provolone. He learned how to slow roast pork from a family-owned restaurant in Rhode Island: brine the meat for six hours, season it, slow roast it for four hours, and then let it cool overnight.

J. K. and his crew aren't afraid to color outside of the lines a little bit. Their 4/20 sandwich, made up of roast beef, pastrami, mustard, cheese, pickled onions, fried eggs, and Cheetos was so popular last April 20 that they brought it back a week later for Willie Nelson's birthday (April 30). Their favorite reaction to the sandwich was a patron proclaiming, "I now know what God eats."

Curry Quinoa Salad

Courtesy of Counter Culture

Sue Davis traded one art form for another when she switched from being a black-and-white fine art printer in the photography world to a chef in vegan restaurants.

1 cup quinoa, rinsed
1½ cups water

Add the quinoa and water to a pot and bring to a boil over high heat. Reduce heat, cover, and simmer for 12 minutes or until the water is absorbed. Fluff with a spoon and transfer to a bowl to cool.

When cool, add:

1 tablespoon curry powder
1 jalapeño, chopped
1 tablespoon fresh ginger, chopped
1 teaspoon salt
¼ cup currants or golden raisins
¼ cup cashews, toasted

Stir to mix. Enjoy at room temperature or chilled.

Counter Culture

A vegetarian since the early 90s and a vegan since 2002, Sue Davis opened the vegan and raw food trailer Counter Culture in July of 2009. One of her favorite things to do is serve an unknowing customer an animal-free dish that they really enjoy, and then tell them it's vegan.

Sweet Sticky Rice

Courtesy of Crepes Mille

With a view of the Texas State Capitol and various upscale bohemian shops, it's always a good time for crepes when you're strolling down South Congress Avenue. This sweet sticky rice belongs with a mango crepe, but it could be coupled with any dish to add a sweet and hearty side. Yield: about 3 cups.

½ cup black glutinous rice
½ cup Thai sticky rice
1¾ cups water, divided
¼ (14-ounce) can coconut milk
¼ teaspoon salt

1 tablespoon brown sugar
2 teaspoons cornstarch dissolved in 2 tablespoons water

1. Soak both rices in 1 cup water for 1 hour.

2. Bring water to gentle boil.

3. Add ¾ cup water, coconut milk , salt, and brown sugar; stir. Add dissolved cornstarch to thicken, and partially cover with lid.

4. Turn the heat down to medium-low and allow to simmer for 20 minutes. Place lid on tight for 10 minutes.

Crepes Mille

Originally from Bangkok, Thailand, Pong Sangritt opened Crepes Mille in May of 2009 to offer savory and sweet Thai-inspired crepes.

One of Pong's favorite parts about the job is meeting so many tourists. "It's like traveling, only we don't move anywhere. I like to talk to people and share experiences. You travel already when you stay right here [at the trailer]."

Banana Nut Bread

Courtesy of The Texas Cuban

Banana lovers will delight in this warm banana nut bread, fresh out of the oven, slathered with butter and toasted to make the edges crispy. Gooey. Buttery. Banana-y. Hurry before it melts off the page. Yield: 1 loaf.

1½ stick butter
1½ cup sugar
2 eggs, beaten with a fork
3 ripe bananas, mashed
2 cups all-purpose flour
1 teaspoon baking soda
Pinch of salt
1 teaspoon vanilla extract
1 cup pecans or almonds, chopped

- Preheat over to 250°F.
- With a mixer, cream butter and sugar until fluffy. Add eggs and bananas, mixing well.
- Combine dry ingredients and stir into banana mixture until moist. Stir in vanilla extract and nuts.
- With a spoon, pour batter into a greased loaf pan.
- Bake for 2 hours.

Mariquitas, Tostones, and Sweet Maduros

Courtesy of The Texas Cuban

Popular in Cuban cuisine, the plantain made its way over from Africa to the tropics, where it became a staple. A little lower in sugar and a bit firmer than a banana, the plantain is the perfect marriage between a banana and a potato. The Cuban treats offered at The Texas Cuban utilize the plantain at all stages: green through nearly black.

Mariquitas
Use green plantains.

Peel green plantains. Slice plantains lengthwise into very thin strips. Fry in oil* until golden brown.

Tostones
Use hard yellow/green plantains.

Peel yellow-green plantains. Slice in round slices. Fry in oil.* Remove and drain on paper towels. Using a brown paper bag, smash the fried slices of plantain flat. Refry. Sprinkle the tostones with salt when done.

Sweet Maduros
Use soft yellow or nearly black plantains.

Peel and slice plantains into semi-thin strips, then cut in half. Fry in oil.*

*Note: Canola oil works best.

Bacon-Wrapped Stuffed Jalapeños

Courtesy of The Sugar Shack BBQ

This is a true Texan appetizer. You can substitute cheddar or string cheese for the cream cheese. Serve just as you're putting the steaks on the grill.

1 pound jalapeños
1 8-ounce brick cream cheese
1 jar of your favorite spicy jelly
1 package bacon
1 package toothpicks

- Cut the jalapeños in half lengthwise and clean out the insides (seeds and veins) using a spoon. Stuff each half with a bit of cream cheese and a bit of jelly.

- Close jalapeños back up and wrap them with half a piece of raw bacon. Stick toothpicks through bacon and stuffed jalapeños. Make sure toothpicks come out the other end. Repeat process until you have stuffed all of the jalapeños.

- Grill assembled jalapeños over medium-high heat. Try to spread them out on the grill because the bacon will cause some flare-ups. Cook until bacon is done, about 20 to 30 minutes

Sugar Shack BBQ

Sugar Shack BBQ was started out of a love for '70s retro music and backyard barbeques by partners Mark Avalos and Mark Stimak. If you're thinking about joining Mark and Mark in the trailer food revolution, they have some words of wisdom: "Don't get fooled by places that have a lot of car traffic. That's the number one misconception. If you see a place that has a ton of cars driving by, you might expect that place to do well, but really, foot traffic is the key." Indeed, Sugar Shack gets plenty of foot traffic at their log-cabin shack on wheels, which is conveniently located just behind Dobie Mall on the UT campus, a favorite place for many students to eat.

Playing with the college environment and their BBQ theme, the trailer's menu includes fun items like the Notorious P.I.G and the Bama Jama. The Sugar Shack's bestseller is the pulled pork with a mustard-base cole slaw, followed closely by their chicken breast sandwich with a white BBQ sauce. White sauce you ask? That's right, the guys at Sugar Shack love all kinds of BBQ, not just Texas-style. Their white sauce is a mayo-based, Alabama-style BBQ sauce with six or seven other ingredients. Not yet available in bottles, their red BBQ sauce is also a fan favorite.

Torchy's Guacamole

Courtesy of Torchy's Tacos

6 ripe avocados, cut into chunks
1 cup white onion, minced
3 tablespoons serrano peppers, minced
1 cup cilantro, chopped
3 tablespoons lime juice
2 teaspoons kosher salt

• Mix all ingredients. Make sure to blend well, but leave chunky and do not over-mix.

Tip: Do not mix with metal or in a metal container; it will cause avocados to turn brown very quickly.

Torchy's Tacos

Ask anyone in Austin where their favorite place to grab a taco is, and you'll likely hear "Torchy's!" in response. Torchy's founding partners are Farrell, Rebecca, and Jay, with Mike Rypka as the chef behind the team. Having worked as a chef at MTV, Dell, Chuy's, Lucy's Boat Yard, and more, putting together delectable flavor combinations with tacos as the vehicle was right up Mike's alley, and his consistently good recipes are the reason behind Torchy's rapid success. In addition to their trailer, they now have multiple brick-and-mortar locations and have expanded into other cities.

Down at the South Austin Trailer Park & Eatery where Torchy's trailer sits, you can enjoy tacos under the shade of the live oak trees that overlook Bouldin Creek. The names of their tacos are equally shady, with such crowd favorites as the Dirty Sanchez. In addition to their normal menu, you can look for specialty items such as their turkey taco with mole during November. What should you get? The Brushfire and the Fried Avocado tacos are hot on my list.

TORCHY'S

DAMN

GOOD

TACOS

CHIPS Y DIPS
CHIPS & SALSA 3⁵⁰
PS & GUACAMOLE 4⁹⁵
GREEN CHILIE QUESO 4⁹⁵
AMOLE, QUESO FRESCO, CILANTRO, AND DIABLO SAUCE

TRAILER PARK
FRIED CHICKEN/GREEN CHILIES/LETTUCE/
PICO DE GALLO/CHEESE 3²⁵
GET IT "TRASHY"-NO LETTUCE/ADD QUESO!

MR. PINK 4⁰⁰
UAJILLO SEARED AHI TUNA/CABBAGE FRESCA/
CILANTRO/QUESO FRESCO/LIME WEDGE

BRUSH FIRE 3⁷⁵
AMAICAN JERK CHICKEN/GRILLED JALAPENOS/
MANGO/SOUR CREAM/CILANTRO

CHICKEN FAJITA 3²⁵
GRILLED CHICKEN BREAST/GRILLED ONIONS
& PEPPERS/CHEESE/PICO DE GALLO

BEEF FAJITA 3⁵⁰
GRILLED SKIRT STEAK/GRILLED ONIONS
& PEPPERS/CHEESE/PICO DE GALLO

DIRTY SANCHEZ 3⁵⁰
SCRAMBLED EGGS/FRIED POBLANO CHILIE/
GUACAMOLE/ESCABECHE CARROTS/
CHEESE

L.B.C.'s Texas Boiled Peanuts

Courtesy of Clem's Hot Diggity Dogs

> **Crack the shell with your teeth and suck the juice like you would the head of a crawfish. Eat the peanut and toss the shell like a boss!**

1 pound raw (green) peanuts
A little less than ¼ cup salt
¼ cup crushed red pepper
⅓ cup dill pickle juice
⅓ cup hot sauce (Big Daddy's Ass Burn from Texas is the ideal choice)
2 large dill pickles, cut in half

- Mix all ingredients in a Crock-Pot and add water until peanuts are covered.
- Heat mixture on high for 4½ hours.
- Reduce heat to low and cook for 5 more hours or until peanuts are tender.

Clem's Hot Diggity Dogs

Brian Clements and best friend, Jason Koon, partnered to develop the Clem's concept and opened their first food cart in February of 2010. Brian's family considers themselves longtime hot-dog connoisseurs, and he has good memories of his dad taking them out to the Howard Johnson's restaurant, where hot dogs were served with square New England lobster rolls. He now uses those same rolls to sandwich Clem's hot dogs.

You might notice the gas-station pricing on the Clem's menu. This is in honor of Brian's grandfather, Clem, who opened a gas station in Virginia Beach after World War II, during the time of nostalgic boardwalks with carnival games. Although Virginia Beach is also where Brian was born, he grew up in Miami. During his time in Florida he developed an affection for the boiled peanut, a treat not readily available in Texas.

Brian claims that Jason is the best friend a guy could have. Jason moved to Austin from the surfing San Diego community. His eight-year-old daughter is their biggest fan, and the guys hope to expand their business to have something to pass down to her and Brian's nephew.

Hummus

Spanish Rice

Courtesy of Bufalo Bob's Chalupa Wagon

This recipe is slightly on the hot side. If you cannot tolerate spicy foods, then cut the cayenne pepper in half. This spread is excellent with blue tortilla chips or pita chips. Yeild: about 2 cups.

2 cups garbanzo beans, cooked
2 tablespoons lemon juice
1 tablespoon tahini
3 tablespoons olive oil
3 tablespoons water
1 tablespoon garlic, minced
1 teaspoon paprika
1 teaspoon cayenne pepper
1 teaspoon Mrs. Dash
  Southwest Chipotle
Pinch of salt

To Cook Garbanzo Beans:
Soak the beans in a bowl with 2 to 3 cups of water per cup of beans for 4 hours. After soaking, add three cups of fresh water for each cup of garbanzo beans in a pot. The liquid should be 1 to 2 inches above the beans. Bring to a boil, reduce heat, and simmer for 1 to 2 hours or until tender.

To Prepare Hummus:
Blend all the ingredients in a food processor until a semi-thick, creamy texture is achieved. It usually takes about 7 to 10 minutes of processing.

With a few key spices you can transform plain rice into a memorable side dish. Yield: about 10 cups.

5 tablespoons olive oil
1 cup chopped onion (½ large onion)
6 teaspoons garlic, minced
2 cups white rice, uncooked
1 cup brown rice, uncooked
7½ cups water
2 cans Rotel Tomatoes & Green Chilies
1 teaspoon sea salt
2 tablespoons parsley
1 tablespoon chili powder

- Heat a large skillet over medium-high heat; add olive oil, chopped onion, and garlic. Cook until onion starts to become translucent (about 10 minutes).
- Add rice and fry for another 10 minutes, until rice starts to brown.
- Add water, Rotel Tomatoes & Green Chilies, and spices. Raise heat until mixture starts to boil; cover and lower to simmer. Cook for another 20 to 25 minutes, or until liquids are absorbed.
- Garnish with more chili powder. Mix and serve.

Sauces, Jams, & Spreads

Bacon Jam

Courtesy of The Peached Tortilla

> This jam is evidence of the Asian/Southern Comfort fusion concept from The Peached Tortilla. Grab your handbasket and serve this spread with whatever you want, whenever you want.

1 pound bacon
4 cloves garlic, chopped
1 brown onion, sliced
2 sprigs fresh thyme
½ cup brewed dark roast coffee
2 tablespoons brown sugar
¼ cup apple cider vinegar

- In cast-iron skillet or pan, lightly brown bacon until crispy.
- Add garlic and onions and cook mixture until onions are opaque.
- Add thyme, coffee, brown sugar, and cider vinegar to mixture and simmer on low heat for 2 hours. If mixture loses moisture, add water.
- After mixture has simmered for 2+ hours, remove thyme sprigs and let mixture cool. Pulse in food processor to desired texture.
- Bacon jam should be spreadable but does not have the texture of preserves or traditional jams.

The Peached Tortilla

Former lawyer Eric Silverstein serves gourmet Asian/Southern American fusion street food from his mobile truck. Born in Japan and having traveled thoroughly around Asia, Eric has been exposed to a variety of cultures and cuisines. At the age of ten, he moved to Atlanta, Georgia, which offered a new range of ingredients and flavors. "When I started [cooking], the concept of mingling Southern and Asian cultures made sense," says Eric. His personal favorite on the menu is the banh mi taco, which includes brined and braised pork belly and is served with a pickled daikon carrot salad sprinkled with sriracha mayo and cilantro.

When asked why he chose the name "Peached Tortilla," Eric says, "It has Georgian roots, because Georgia's the peach state. The word 'peached' allows you to define it yourself. To us, 'peached' is to get flavor-smitten—we want people to get 'peached.' The tortilla ties in with tacos. We also want to separate ourselves out from corporate America, and this name was one way to do that."

Eric represents the rebel version of entrepreneurs who aren't satisfied working for someone else. After discussing a new city with his girlfriend and researching his concept extensively, Eric quit his job and three weeks later they moved to Austin and opened The Peached Tortilla. Why Austin? "We felt like it was a really open-minded city where people would be comfortable trying out food from a truck. There was already a tremendous amount of growth in the trailer food industry, the city is growing, the economy is doing well, my concept is different, and Austin likes different." Currently, Eric is dishing up his gourmet fusion cuisine at multiple locations.

Onion Marmalade

Courtesy of The Jalopy

An earthy, warm, yet herbal-fresh marmalade you can slather on meats or breads. Or beards.

5 red onions, julienned
Butter
¾ bottle dry red wine
2 cups high-quality balsamic vinegar
2 sticks cinnamon
2 teaspoons allspice berries
1 tablespoon ground cloves
1 tablespoon fresh nutmeg
1 tablespoon freshly ground black pepper
1 cup cane sugar
Salt to taste

- In a large pot, cook onions with butter over low heat for 20 minutes, or until they become translucent.
- In a separate pot, heat wine and vinegar and reduce by about 75 percent. Mix in cinnamon, allspice berries, ground cloves, nutmeg, and pepper. Add the reduction to the onions.
- Let simmer for 5 minutes, then add cane sugar.
- Let simmer for another 5 minutes, then add salt to taste.

The Jalopy

When Nick Patrizi graduated from the University of Texas, his family was very serious when they sat him down and told him he could do anything he wanted except something in the food and beverage industry. After all, coming from a large Italian family with a history of owning restaurants, they knew firsthand the ups and downs of the restaurant business. Yet instead of taking on corporate finance banking gigs, Nick decided to try his hand at the family business. But he did it his own way—out of a trailer.

The contrast of clean, quality product with super-friendly Nick in a white chef coat working out of an old eighteen wheeler is beautiful. He uses onion marmalade with reduced red wine, reduced balsamic, and clove in a demi-glace to sauce up his chicken. He boils down chicken bones in a huge pot to make chicken butter, which takes seventy-two hours to make. He also serves an Asian-inspired sauce with oyster and sweet chile. My favorite part of our ingredient discussion was when he said, "We have seven different peppers that I pickle (that's a peck): anaheims, poblanos, hatch, serranos, etc." For his Asian chicken hot sandwiches he toasts and caramelizes the bread so there is a little burned factor to it, just like at home. In case your mouth isn't watering yet, he also offers a caprese sandwich, but instead of basil he uses a juicy, spicy parsley pesto with a medley of six different nuts (not quite a peck), lemon juice, serranos, garlic, and olive oil.

Mole Rojo

Courtesy of El Naranjo

It is said that no two moles are alike, and a mole is a bit of a mystery sauce. Iliana of El Naranjo told me there are more than two hundred traditional moles in Mexico to choose from, but she gave us her best one for this recipe. You can use this in enchiladas or as a sauce for meats or grilled veggies. (See the note below on how Iliana cooks chicken to accompany this authentic sauce.) Yield: 16 servings.

1 pound tomatoes
1 large white onion
8 medium garlic cloves, unpeeled
½ pound ancho chiles
¼ pound guajillo chiles
3 tablespoons vegetable oil, divided
2 ounces pecans
2 ounces unsalted peanuts, roasted
2-inch stick of Mexican canela (cinnamon)
4 tablespoons brown sesame seeds
1 tablespoon dried Mexican oregano or marjoram
8 black peppercorns
4 whole cloves
1½ cups chicken broth

Sugar to taste (approximately 2 tablespoons)
7 ounces Mexican chocolate
Salt to taste

Chicken Broth
16 assorted chicken pieces*
½ white onion
4 garlic cloves

- On a comal or griddle over medium-high heat, dry roast the tomatoes, onion, and unpeeled garlic. The garlic will be done first; when it shows brown spots, remove.
- Remove the stems, seeds, and veins from the chiles, then dry roast them on a dry comal; transfer to soak in hot water for no more than 15 minutes.
- Heat 1½ tablespoons oil in a skillet and sauté the pecans and peanuts. When the nuts are golden, add the canela, sesame seeds, oregano, peppercorns, and cloves. Mix and remove from heat.
- Transfer the chiles to a blender. Add enough water to blend; process until smooth. Strain and reserve.
- Heat remaining oil in a large cazuela (Dutch oven) over medium-low heat. Pour the chile puree over the oil and fry for 5 to 10 minutes.
- Blend the tomatoes, onion, and garlic, then pass through a sieve. Stir into the chile paste, let the mole reduce, and then add the chicken broth, sugar, chocolate, and salt to taste. Simmer, stirring occasionally, until the mole is thick enough to cover the back of a spoon.

* To cook the chicken: In a large stockpot, bring salted water to a boil, add onion and garlic. When the water reaches a full boil, add the chicken pieces with bones and skins. Reduce the heat to low; let the chicken cook until done (it will be floating on top). Check for doneness, remove, and reserve. Strain the broth and reserve for the mole.

El Naranjo

Before calling Austin home, Iliana de la Vega and Ernesto Torrealba
had a restaurant in Oaxaca, Mexico, which they opened in 1997. When
turmoil upset their local economy in 2006, the couple moved stateside
to continue the family business. Iliana says, "We picked Austin
because we have friends here, and it's a city I like. It's hard when you
leave your own country, but I feel really welcome in Austin with the
community. I can call it my home. It's green and beautiful, and the
people are nice and laid back."

Even though it's a complicated food to serve from the trailer,
Iliana most enjoys preparing the mole. "It is basically a sauce that is
itself a dish. You have to have dried or fresh chiles and a thickener
component, plus some spices. Chile is a vegetable not a spice."
Before arriving at the trailer in the afternoons, Iliana works as a
Mexican cuisine specialist at the Culinary Institute of America in
San Antonio. She is currently creating an archive of rare recipes for
common street foods in Latin America and Mexico that also includes
anthropological and cooking data in video and print formats.

That's Amore Olive Tapenade

Courtesy of That's Amore

This tapenade is good enough to eat with a spoon. You might also try it on bell peppers or on crostinis with Parmesan. That's Amore owner Angela uses it as a spread for the Pizzo Panini, which includes mortadella, salami, smoked ham, provolone, Italian roasted tomatoes, and, of course, this olive tapenade.

1 cup pitted kalamata olives
1 cup green olives stuffed with pimiento
½ cup roasted red peppers
2 cloves fresh garlic
1 tablespoon each of dry herbs: thyme, basil, oregano
3 tablespoons freshly squeezed lemon juice
¼ cup extra-virgin olive oil
½ teaspoon fresh cracked black pepper

• Thoroughly rinse olives in cool water. Place ingredients in food processor. Pulse until mixture becomes coarsely blended (approximately 2 to 3 minutes).

Sauce Andalouse

Courtesy of Frietkot

Inspired by French-fry food trailers setting up outside of bars in Belgium, Eric and Marc use fries as a canvas for multiple sides and toppings. This is one of them. Serve with Belgian fries, sandwiches, or anything you feel a tasty condiment would complement. Yield: 4 to 6 servings.

5 egg yolks
1½ tablespoons water
4 cloves garlic
1 small shallot, minced
2 tablespoons Dijon mustard
1 shot sriracha
2 lemons, juiced
1 red bell pepper, minced
½ cup basil leaves, torn
¼ cup parsley, chopped
1 cup vegetable or
  grapeseed oil
Kosher salt to taste
Freshly cracked black
  pepper to taste

- Mix all ingredients except oil, salt, and pepper in a food processor until blended.
- Slowly add oil to running processor in a steady stream until mixture starts to thicken. The mixture should be of a mayo-like consistency, light red in color, and have some texture.
- Season mixture with salt and pepper to taste, remove from food processor, and store in an airtight container, refrigerated, for up to 5 days.

Frietkot

Eric Wolf, owner of Lovejoy's in downtown Austin, opened his Frietkot fries trailer in 2010 after much market research and development. While in Belgium, he noticed that there were multiple fry stands outside of bars, with long lines of people waiting for late-night snacks. In his words, the French-fry trailers were a "cool, simple idea, and also something that went well with the bar scene." Plus, he and his friends usually eat at trailers more often than brick-and-mortar restaurants, so opening a trailer restaurant made sense. Eric's personal favorite sauce at the trailer is the garlic aioli, though the bacon aioli is their bestseller.

Hollandaise Sauce

Courtesy of Crepes Mille

Hollandaise always seems better when someone else makes it for you, but now you can make it at home. Or better yet, someone at home can make it for you!

½ cup unsalted butter
2 tablespoons fresh lemon juice
¼ teaspoon cracked peppe corns
3 large egg yolks
½ teaspoon salt

- Melt the butter and keep it warm.
- Heat lemon juice and peppercorns until nearly dry.
- In a double boiler over hot water, whisk egg yolks together until thickened. Do not let yolks get so hot that they scramble.
- Gradually add butter, lemon juice, and salt.

Organic Fig Spread

Courtesy of La Boîte

Use this unique and mysterious spread from French-inspired trailer La Boîte to liven up sandwiches or toast.

1 pound organic dried figs
3 cups red wine
Pinch of cinnamon

- Remove fig stalks. Place figs in a saucepan with the wine and cinnamon.
- Bring to a boil and then simmer 10 minutes, or until the figs are hydrated and pulpy.
- Place figs and half of the liquid into a food processor and blend. Add additional liquid until the consistency of the spread is a little thicker than a jam.

La Boîte Café

La Boîte Café is a beautifully built-out shipping container nestled on the grassy hillside of the 1700 South Lamar shopping area. Victoria, with her New Zealand accent, and her partner, Dan, met in Austin and started working on the La Boîte concept in the beginning of 2009 as an escape from the corporate life. Their repurposed container is a walk-in rather than walk-up trailer, and their rainwater collection and purification system is highly credible among the environmentally concerned. The menu has a bistro feel with multiple items from our local Austin farmers, including Pederson, Richardson, and Full Quiver Farms. Stop in for a chocolate-vanilla coffee and croissant for breakfast, or a fresh, locally made artisan sandwich with a colorful macaroon for lunch.

Chipotle Mayo

Courtesy of Moo Moo's Mini Burgers

Use this artisan mayo as a spread on sandwiches and grilled vegetables.

Canned chipotle peppers in
  adobe sauce
Mayonnaise

• Add two chipotle peppers plus 1 tablespoon of adobe sauce to 1 cup of mayo. Blend in a blender. Adjust level of spiciness to taste.

Spicy Peanut Sauce

Courtesy of The Jalopy

You know these trailer food chefs—making up sauces, not knowing how much of what, every batch is different. Don't be skeerd.

Sweet chili sauce
Peanut butter
Sriracha
Heavy cream

Sesame oil
Rice wine vinegar
Salt and pepper to taste

Blend and chill. Garnish and use as a dipping sauce. You can also use this sauce with pasta, or spread it on a sandwich.

Homemade Ketchup

Courtesy of Along Came a Slider

Along Came a Slider has quite the following for its homemade ketchup.

½ cup brown sugar
½ cup sugar
2 tablespoons onion powder
2 tablespoons garlic powder
1 teaspoon cayenne
¼ cup salt
2 tablespoons pepper
½ cup red wine vinegar

½ cup apple cider vinegar
½ cup balsamic vinegar
12 cups diced tomatoes (10-pound can or 96 ounces)

- In a large pot, combine all ingredients and bring to a boil.
- Reduce heat and simmer until thickened (approximately 45 minutes).
- Blend in a food processor.

Along Came a Slider

Business partners Tyler Johnson and Jeff Shaver have combined service-industry experience including dish washing, waiting tables, bar tending and bar management, attending culinary school, and working as an executive sous chef. The concept for Along Came a Slider includes using sustainable, local organic products and the meat of humanely raised animals. As the partners describe, "We see sliders as being the perfect vehicle for any dish—classic French, Asian, Mexican, and beyond."

Onions-n-Sauce

Courtesy of Big Top Dogs

If you can't get New York favorite Sabrett's version, you can make this sauce at home to top your dogs.

1½ teaspoon olive oil
2 medium onions, sliced thin and chopped
3 cups water
2 tablespoons tomato paste
2 teaspoons corn syrup
1 teaspoon cornstarch
½ teaspoon salt
¼ cup crushed red pepper flakes
¼ cup vinegar

- Heat the oil in a large saucepan over medium heat. Sauté onions in oil for 5 minutes, until onions are soft but not brown.
- Add water, tomato paste, corn syrup, cornstarch and salt; stir. Bring to a boil, then reduce heat and simmer for 45 minutes.
- Add red pepper flakes and vinegar. Continue to simmer for an additional 30 to 45 minutes or until most of the liquid has reduced and the sauce is thick.

Big Top Dogs

Long before John Dawson had his hands on the mobile vending scene, his grandfather was selling peanuts from a pushcart in Toledo, Ohio. A Greek immigrant coming through Ellis Island at age sixteen, his granddad eventually developed his street food business into the brick-and-mortar restaurant/diner Clean Bite in Toledo, Ohio, where John's mother spent time as a waitress during the Depression and war years. It was a bit of fate that John would develop Big Top Dogs after living in New York, where his grandfather started their family's journey to pursue the American dream.

A Day Trip to the Trailers: Downtown & Campus

Home to the State Capitol, the sprawling University of Texas campus, the legendary 6th Street, and a trendy new warehouse district, Austin's center boasts multiple cuisines, from traditional American classics like BBQ and burgers to international indulgences like kebabs and Indian fare.

You'll want to try Hot Dog King (8th and Red River), with lots of dog options including great vegetarian choices, as well as Patika Coffee (2nd and Congress), which is the perfect downtown pick-me-up. If you're near campus, check out the Cajun delights—especially the po' boys and étouffée—of Lee's Hurricane Party (Martin Luther King Jr. and Rio Grande) and the Asian street food of Fresh Off the Truck (20th and Whitis).

Just adjacent to the university is the Drag (Guadalupe Street), where you can do some shopping and people-watching at both freestanding artist kiosks and brick-and-mortar boutiques. The Drag will give you a true picture of Austin, with its graffiti murals, college students, funky art and jewelry, and high-end dress and gift shops.

Other notable stops downtown include the Bob Bullock Texas State History Museum (with Imax theatre inside), The Paramount Theatre (originally called The Majestic when it opened in 1915), the Blanton Museum of Art, the Austin Museum of Art, and the Austin Children's Museum.

While you're in the area, be sure to check out local alt-weekly *The Chronicle* for music listings. Try Antone's, a local institution and Austin's home of the blues. Other music venues within walking distance include La Zona Rosa and the Austin Music Hall. My personal favorite, a little west of downtown, is Donn's Depot, where Donn Adleman himself tickles the ivories every Tuesday and Friday night, playing outlaw country music spiced with Elvis and classic rock. You'll find all-ages boot-scooting until two in the morning. (If you're a woman, check out the famous ladies room).

Head further west for a few more favorites. The Mean Eyed Cat is a tribute bar honoring the one and only Johnny Cash, and Deep Eddy Cabaret is a beer bar with some pool tables. It's located right next to Deep Eddy pool, a public swimming hole fed with natural spring water.

Tacos

Sandwiches

Burgers

Other Handheld Gourmet Street Food Lunches

Cherry Wood Smoked Catfish Tacos

Courtesy of Smokilicious Bar-B-Q

Smoke-cooking fish is fast and easy and cherry wood goes well with catfish. If you've no time to brine, a quick, savory, and flavorful rub will give a kick to your fillet. Yield: 8 large fillets.

Rub Ingredients:
1 tablespoon yellow mustard
1 tablespoon salt
1 tablespoon black pepper
2 teaspoon lemon pepper
2 teaspoon thyme
1 teaspoon paprika
1 teaspoon light chili powder

Fixings to build the taco:
8 catfish fillets
Warm corn tortillas
Lettuce, shredded
Red cabbage, shredded
Carrots, shredded
Tomatoes, cubed
Onions, diced
Cilantro, chopped
Jalapeños, sliced

- Remove any silver skin from catfish fillets, rinse with cold water, and pat dry with paper towel.
- Lightly rub yellow mustard on both sides of fillets. Mix all dry ingredients together and sprinkle liberally on both sides. Place fillets on rack or sheet pan and allow to rest while preparing the smoker.
- If you use a barrel pit, grill, or another type of smoker, prepare as usual and hold temperature between 190°F and 200°F. Do not cover grates with foil, as this will allow moisture to settle under the fish and leave a thin, slimy film on the bottom of the fillet. Whatever you use, get to know your smoker or grill, how it cooks, how it holds heat, etc.
- Load the cherry wood chips and place the fish on the grates, leaving enough room between the fillets to allow the heat and smoke to move freely around each one, so that the fish will cook evenly.
- Depending on the smoker and the thickness of the fillets, it should only take about 1 to 1½ hours at 190°F to fully cook the fillets. When cooked, remove fillets, cover with foil, and let stand for 10 to 15 minutes before serving.
- Serve on warm corn tortillas with lettuce, red cabbage, carrots, tomatoes, onions, cilantro, and jalapeños.

Royito's Soft Chicken Tacos

Courtesy of Royito's Hot Sauce Streamer

Choosy moms choose Royito's soft chicken tacos. For breakfast, lunch, or dinner, these are easy to make and taste so good. Yield: 8 tacos.

1 tablespoon olive oil or other cooking oil
1 pound skinless/boneless chicken breasts, cut into strips
Royito's Hot Sauce to taste
Mexican cheese
8 flour tortillas

- In a sauté pan, heat oil and cook chicken strips until completely done.
- Add Royito's Hot Sauce and lightly simmer for 5 to 10 minutes, turning as needed.
- Arrange the Royito's-cooked chicken slices on the flour tortillas and sprinkle with your favorite Mexican cheese. *Sabor!*

Korean Bulgogi Taco

Courtesy of Chi'Lantro

Chi'Lantro is Austin's version of the Korean barbecue truck. The Korean bulgogi taco is one of their bestsellers, and this is the beef version.

Beef Taco Filling:
2 pounds thinly sliced beef rib eye
14 tablespoons soy sauce
2 tablespoons vinegar
4 tablespoons white sugar
2 tablespoons garlic, minced
1 teaspoon ginger, minced
1 yellow onion, diced
2 teaspoons sesame oil
Corn or flour tortillas (4.5 inch)

Korean Vinaigrette Salad:
Napa cabbage
Green leaf lettuce
½ cup soy sauce
¼ cup rice vinegar
¼ cup sugar
3 cups water
4 tablespoons sesame oil
Onions, chopped
Cilantro, chopped
Korean pepper
Korean–Mexican salsa
Sesame seeds

- Marinate the meat for 24 hours in the combined soy sauce, vinegar, sugar, garlic, ginger, onion, and sesame oil. Cook the meat shortly before serving.
- For the salad, shred the cabbage and lettuce. Make a dressing with the rest of the ingredients.
- To serve, fill tacos with salad and top with meat.

Chi'Lantro BBQ

Born in Korea and raised in Orange County, California, Jae grew up eating burritos and Korean food. Culturally diverse Austin, with its large population of Koreans and Mexicans, seemed the perfect place to open a business that straddles the two cultures. After refining his recipes based on the feedback of friends and family, Jae opened his Kor'exican taco truck.

Fried Egg Tuna Melt with Jalapeños, Cranberries, and Walnuts

Courtesy of The Local Yolk

Like your mom, Shelly of The Local Yolk doesn't cook with precise amounts. So you'll just have to experiment with the ingredients she provided to taste, to create your own version of this Local Yolk favorite.

White albacore tuna
Greek plain yogurt (instead of mayo)
Dijon mustard
Celery
Lemon juice
Purple onion
Jalapeño
Dried cranberries
Crushed walnuts
Sea salt
Cracked black pepper

- Stir it all up and put it in between the bread of your choice.
- Add a slice of mozzarella cheese and a fried egg, and grill to perfection!

Local Yolk

Having catered, bartended, and waited tables, Shelly Speer was a natural for the trailer food business. Her menu concept is centered entirely on the incredible edible egg. "I just really love to make egg sandwiches. It's fun to see how many different ones I can come up with." Her personal favorite is the tuna melt that comes with a fried egg on top. The Florence is a crowd favorite; it's an Italian grilled sandwich with pesto, tomato, mozzarella, and a fried egg. She also sells deviled eggs with curry singly or by the dozen, and she anticipates adding other engaging, fun flavors to change things up.

Shelly doesn't have her own chickens yet, so she buys her eggs from Farm to Table. All of her sandwiches come with Kettle chips and a pickle. She developed her French toast dessert snack when a cinnamon swirl loaf was accidentally delivered instead of her normal sandwich bread: "I made French toast, and we passed it out for free for people to try, and everyone loved it. I cut it into squares and drizzle syrup over it with a toothpick. It's good for a late-night snack or brunch."

Turkey and Brie Sandwich with Organic Fig Spread

Courtesy of La Boîte

This is one of La Boîte's most popular sandwich combinations. The key is to use a good creamy Brie and an extra soft bread roll. The sandwich is wonderful heated in the oven.

3–4 ounces sliced organic turkey
4 ounces Brie
Organic fig spread (see page 71)
Fresh baked bread roll

- Slice the roll lengthwise and spread liberally with fig spread. Add turkey and Brie. Heat briefly in the oven if desired, and serve.

Gadd Thai Sandwich

Courtesy of The Jalopy

Good Gadd, you're going to love this. Talk amongst yourselves.

2 slices bread, toasted
3 ounces rotisserie chicken (see rotisserie chicken recipe under Dinner)
Pickled red onions
Fresh parsley
Fresh cilantro
Red cabbage, julienned
Scallions
Spicy peanut sauce (See Sauces, Jams, & Spreads)

- Arrange chicken and all ingredients between toasted bread slices.
- Press the completed sandwich to caramelize the toast and heat the fillings.
- Fried chicken skin can be added for extra crunch . . . nom nom nom.

Pork Banh Mi

Courtesy of Me So Hungry

The pork banh mi is the "burger" of fusion trailer food. Here is everything you need to make your own at home. Just one thing—how do you make sweet cilantro mayonnaise?

Start with Mexican French bread and cover it in sweet cilantro mayonnaise. Add:

BBQ pork
Fresh cucumber, julienned
Jalapeños, chopped
Pickled carrots
Cilantro
Sriracha hot sauce to taste

Sweet Cilantro Mayo:
2 tablespoons sugar
1 tablespoon cilantro
1 cup mayo

Me So Hungry

Christina Alonso, previously in interior design, opened Me So Hungry in January of 2009. Her unique culinary concept evolved from a blend of the flavors she grew up with. Christina's mother had a large role in the startup by contributing her peanut sauce recipe as well as the name of the trailer: she speaks seven languages, and "me so hungry" is one of her endearing phrases.

Christina and fans adore their pork *banh mi*. This sandwich is made on Mexican French Bread (*pain français*), covered in sweet cilantro mayonnaise (made fresh every morning), BBQ pork, fresh cucumber, jalapeños, pickled carrots, cilantro, and hot sauce. The Sweet Shroom sandwich is the vegetarian bestseller and consists of Jewish rye covered in homemade vegan Sadie sauce, portabella mushrooms sautéed with sweet chile and olive oil, Chinese BBQ sauce, fried egg, fresh sprouts, greens, carrots, cilantro, and hot sauce.

#19 Cheesesteak

Courtesy of #19 Bus

Cut in half and enjoy with some chips and a pickle spear. Goes great with Lone Star beer!

3 ounces red and green bell peppers (1½ ounces each)
1½ ounces white onions
Olive oil
1½ ounces sliced mushrooms
Salt and pepper to taste
6 ounces thinly sliced sirloin (slightly thicker than paper)
10-inch Amoroso roll (or hoagie roll)
2 slices white American cheese

- Thinly slice bell peppers and onions.
- Roast peppers in olive oil; season with salt and pepper.
- Lightly sauté the mushrooms in a small amount of oil; season with salt and pepper.
- Turn heat up, and on a flat grill, griddle, or large skillet, throw the thinly sliced sirloin and start immediately separating the meat and cooking to a nice light brown. You want a hot cooking surface!
- Slice the hoagie roll and lightly coat with butter. If you have the room, throw the roll face down on the griddle; otherwise, put it into an oven on broil.
- Throw in roasted red bell peppers, then an equal amount of green bell peppers.
- Toss in the mushrooms with peppers and meat. Cook until meat is cooked through, making sure not to overcook meat.
- Add salt and pepper to taste and mix.
- Line up mixture on griddle so that it will fit on roll.
- Throw two slices of cheese on top and squirt water around edges to create a steaming effect. This will melt the cheese faster. Remember, you don't want to overcook the thinly sliced sirloin.
- Once cheese is melted, grab toasted roll and drop it face down on mix. With a long spatula, scoop and turn mixture onto roll. It is very important to time this perfectly. It is easy to overcook this sandwich.

#19 Bus

Having worked in an engineering firm, owned a hair salon, and managed a deli, Tim Lasater's background is as colorful as it is diverse. During his last tour through Philly with his band, Pop Unknown, he realized no one served really good cheesesteak in Austin. That's when he decided to enter the trailer food business. Fate led him to the only factory-made double-decker bus in the United States, which was originally built as a tour bus for the Cheshire Inn, a hotel in Saint Louis, in 1975.

Tim wanted to name the business something simple that everyone could remember, so he chose "#19 Bus" after The Clash's song about a double-decker bus in Britain that carried people home from live music venues and bars. The name seemed a natural fit.

Wurst Tex

Without a wealth of culinary expertise, Sam Raver and fiancée, Leslie Coffey, along with Sam's step-dad, set out to begin a new chapter in their lives. They developed a straightforward sausage concept for their first shot at the trailer food business. Their menu of exotic game sausages, however, is miles from the standard bratwurst experience. From rattlesnake and venison, to rabbit and duck, to more regular sausages and extraordinary vegetarian options, the Wurst Tex menu is truly unique.

The Predator and Prey, which contains rattlesnake, rabbit, and pork with jalapeños, is Sam's personal favorite.

Two fun "sausage" options for vegetarians are the 04 Delight, a combination of smoked apples, sage, and potatoes, and the Veggiano, which contains eggplant, fennel, and garlic.

Wurst Tex Gourmet Sausage Sandwich

Courtesy of Wurst Tex

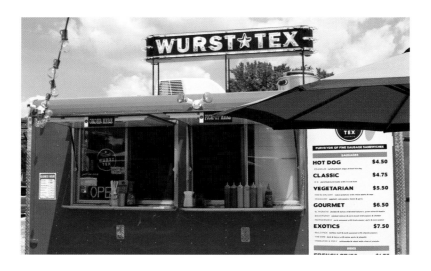

This gourmet festival fare is perfect to serve to guests watching a game, during a backyard birthday party, or when grilling for a campout.

1 jalapeño
½ red bell pepper
½ onion
¼ cup sauerkraut
1 fresh-baked bun (never use day-old bread)
1 tablespoon of herb butter, melted
Salt and pepper
1 link of your favorite sausage

- Clean and gut jalapeño, then slice.
- Slice red pepper and onion and set aside.
- On stove, heat sauerkraut over low to medium heat until warm. Melt herb butter in a separate pan.
- On grill, place onion in sheet of foil, season with salt and pepper, wrap up, and put over low heat on grill.
- Place red bell pepper and jalapeño in sheet of foil, season with salt and pepper, wrap up, and put over low heat on grill.
- Lightly coat fresh-baked bun with melted herb butter, wrap in foil, and place over low heat on grill.
- Add sausage link to grill, brush with butter, and cook until 165°F and golden brown.
- Take bun out of foil and lightly touch to grill on front and back.
- To assemble, place sausage in bun and top with sauerkraut, grilled onions, and peppers. Dress with mustards and ketchups of choice. We recommend trying spicy brown mustard and curry ketchup.

Barbacoa-Style Brisket Slider

Courtesy of Along Came a Slider

This recipe from slider specialists Tyler and Jeff of Along Came a Slider makes enough for a small party. The leftovers will be even better the next day.

Barbacoa-Style Brisket:

1 yellow onion, chopped
1 jalapeño, chopped
2 ancho chiles, toasted and seeded
2 guajillo chiles, toasted and seeded
1 bunch cilantro, chopped
1 cup apple cider vinegar
¼ cup salt
10 pounds beef brisket

1. Blend all ingredients except brisket until a smooth puree is achieved.

2. Cut brisket into 2-inch cubes and toss with puree.

3. Process on high pressure in a pressure cooker for 90 minutes. (Alternatively, braise in oven at 300°F until falling apart, approximately 8 hours.)

4. Shred brisket and toss with cooking liquid.

5. Season to taste with salt and pepper.

Pickled Red Onions:

1 cup red wine vinegar
1 cup sugar
2 red onions, thinly sliced

1. Bring vinegar and sugar to a boil.

2. Pour over red onions and let sit at room temperature for 1 hour.

3. Refrigerate.

Lime-Infused Crema:

1 cup Mexican crema
1 lime, zested and juiced
Salt and pepper to taste

1. Combine crema, lime juice, and lime zest.

2. Season to taste with salt and pepper.

To build the slider, place the brisket on fresh baked buns and top it with pickled onions, fresh cilantro, and lime-infused crema.

Grilled Portabella Mushroom Burger

Moo Moo's Mini Burgers

This delicious and healthy burger is served with grilled onions, avocados, and chipotle mayo.

Portabella mushroom (choose one larger than the bun)
Olive Oil
Onions
Salt and pepper to taste
Swiss cheese
Fresh-baked bun
Avocado
Chipotle Mayo (see page 73)

- Remove stem from portabella and clean out. Brush each side with olive oil.
- Grill each side for 4 to 5 minutes, starting with the cap up. Mushroom will shrink and become soft. Grill the last 30 seconds with the bottom part up.
- Slice up some onions, drizzle them with olive oil, and sprinkle with salt and pepper to taste. Sauté until onions become soft and caramelized.
- Stuff mushroom cavity with the grilled onions and top with Swiss cheese. Let cheese melt.
- Toast bun. Add avocado and Chipotle Mayo on bottom half of bun. Add mushroom. Top with the other bun half and enjoy.

Downtown Burgers

Born in New York and raised in Chicago, Steve McDermott has lived in eight states and spent more than forty years working in nearly every genre of food in the restaurant industry. Steve says, "My mother was Greek, and she and my grandparents and aunts always cooked, so it's in my blood." Among his other restaurant victories, he once owned The Original Chicago Pizza Company in Lake Geneva, Wisconsin. Additionally, he spent some time with the Austin icon El Arroyo.

Steve initially set up office for an e-car rental business out of a trailer, but the city shut it down. He then decided to sell something from his trailer that the city would allow: burgers. Steve's attitude? "If you can't beat 'em, you might as well join 'em."

One-Pound Bacon Cheeseburger

Courtesy of Downtown Burgers

All the way please.

4 strips apple smoked bacon
1 4½-inch sesame seed bun
4 4-ounce 80/20 fresh ground
   beef patties
4 1-ounce slices cheddar cheese
Ketchup
Mustard
Mayo
3 jalapeño slices
3 slices red onion
3 dill pickle chips
3 leaves iceberg lettuce
3 slices roma tomato

- Grill bacon.
- Cook beef patties on a
  charcoal grill.
- Add cheese and bacon to the
  burgers on the grill.
- Toast bun.
- Apply ketchup, mustard, and
  mayo to bottom buns.
- Add jalapeños, onions, and
  pickles to bottom buns.
- Stack beef patties.
- Add lettuce and tomatoes.
- Place top bun . . .

Hat Creek Cheeseburger

Courtesy of Hat Creek Burger Company

Drew Gressett of Hat Creek Burger Company uses all-natural Black Angus beef patties that are never frozen in his version of this American classic.

Black Angus beef patties
Hat Creek special seasoning
Slices of cheese, your choice (American if you take Drew's recommendation)
Fresh-baked buns
Ketchup

- While the patties are on the grill, top them with Hat Creek's special seasoning (don't overdo it) and a slice of cheese. Put the juicy patty on a slightly toasted bun to create an incredible cheeseburger that is one of the best around.

Hat Creek Burger Co.

Hometown hero Drew Gressett grew up in Austin and graduated from the University of Texas before doing a fair amount of traveling between Washington, DC, Dallas, and China with a real estate venture. He'd always had a dream of owning a hamburger stand, and in 2008, he decided it was now or never. So he opened Hat Creek Burgers. He's had no regrets.

Drew says his mom taught him how to make his first burger. "She always cooked a typical backyard burger with a thick patty. Ours are thinner. Manageability of a smaller burger, that's our angle at Hat Creek." His favorite way to eat a Big Hat burger is with American cheese and ketchup only. Burger sizes are indicated by hat sizes: the Big Hat has two fifth-pound patties and the Little Hat has one fifth-pound patty. They offer four cheeses to choose from: American, Cheddar, Pepper Jack, and Swiss. Drew says the premise of their product is a super-fresh, hand-pattied burger whose meat has never seen a freezer. "Freezers are for ice cream," he says. His burgers contain fresh-cracked pepper and all-natural, hormone- and antibiotic-free, vegetarian-fed beef.

Though Hat Creek started out as a trailer, Drew moved it into a brick-and-mortar building in 2009 and now uses the trailer for special events, such as making burgers for fans at UT baseball games. Drew makes a good point when he says that "the mobile trailer is such a great platform to eventually get into a brick-and-mortar, and then for a brick-and-mortar, it's good to expand business with a mobile unit." UT basketball coach Rick Barnes and football coach Mac Brown are among two of Drew's guests. His employees love the burgers so much that one of them regularly enjoys eating a ten-patty Big Hat after clocking out.

Hot 'n' Crunchy Chicken

Courtesy of The Mighty Cone

Lowbrow fun, with a highbrow attitude.

¼ cup almonds
¼ cup sesame seeds
2 cups corn flakes
¼ cup granulated sugar
1½ tablespoon red chili flakes
1 tablespoon salt
2 cups flour
Egg wash (4 fresh eggs and 1½ cups milk whisked together)
8 chicken tenders
1 quart of vegetable oil for frying

- Put all the above ingredients, except the chicken and cooking oil, in a food processor with an S blade and pulse lightly until combined, keeping it coarse and not overly processed.
- Set up a standard breading procedure station—flour to egg wash to breading—in three similar-sized pans.
- Coat each chicken tender in the flour, until well dusted. Pat off excess flour.
- Pass dusted chicken tender through the egg wash, wetting completely.
- Place the chicken tender in the hot and crunchy mixture and cover with crumbs, lightly pressing the mixture onto the tender with the palm of your hand. Remove and shake off excess mixture.
- Set aside on a dry sheet pan or cookie sheet until all of the chicken tenders are breaded.
- In a large, heavy sauté pan, heat 1 quart of vegetable oil to 350°F.
- Lay the chicken tenders in the hot oil and deep fry for about 3 minutes. They will cook to a golden, crunchy brown if the pan is at the right temperature.
- Place on a cookie sheet or pan in a 150°F oven until you have completed the frying process for all of the tenders.

The Mighty Cone

Jeff Blank had owned Hudson's on the Bend for over twenty-five years before making a debut in the street food scene. Having achieved mad success at the Austin City Limits Music Festival for eight consecutive years with The Mighty Cone, he thought he would open a trailer to see how it was accepted. And accepted it was. People like the Hudson's quality but appreciate the Mighty Cone's low price. In fact, there have been sightings of people at Hudson's on a Friday night who then show up at The Mighty Cone for Saturday lunch (in the same clothes). Some folks just can't stay away from a Hudson's-prepped meal.

Jeff's favorite part about the business? "We have lowbrow fun with a highbrow attitude." The bestselling chicken and avocado cone is his personal favorite. But what exactly is a Mighty Cone? This street food concept was developed to give festival-goers a tasty yet inexpensive food option. Jeff teamed up with Hudson's Executive Chef Robert Rhodes to create a unique batter for the chicken, which they wrapped in a tortilla and dropped into a paper drink cone. While they have a variety of toppings, the original Hot 'n' Crunchy Chicken Cone comes with a mango-jalapeño slaw and ancho sauce. How could you refuse this fusion of Southern-fried goodness, Mexican flare, and ease on the pocketbook for a hefty meal you can walk around with?

The Bird Dog

Courtesy of Man Bites Dog

> **Bk-gok! Chicken sausage link with pesto mayo-y goodness and sweet corn relish. Order up!**

⅓ cup white vinegar
½ cup sugar
¼ teaspoon dry mustard
¼ teaspoon garlic powder
¼ cup onion, diced
4 tablespoons red and green pepper, diced
1 15-ounce can yellow whole-kernel corn
Chicken sausage
1 awesome hot dog bun

Pesto mayo (half mayo, half basil pesto)

- Combine vinegar, sugar, mustard, garlic powder, and onion in a pan, and bring to a simmer.
- Add peppers and corn and stir for about 10 minutes, then cool.
- Cook chicken sausage over a grill or griddle.
- Assemble by putting the dog in the bun, zig-zagging with mayo, and piling on your homemade relish.

Man Bites Dog

With an MBA and twelve years of restaurant experience, Jeremiah opened the first Man Bites Dog trailer in November of 2009 and the second in March of 2010. After spending some time in Chicago, he decided there wasn't anything like the dogs back in Austin, so he put together some forty-odd variations around a hot dog theme and narrowed the menu down to twelve of his favorite combinations. The Buffalo Hottie, which won the Critics' Choice Award for the best nontraditional hot dog in the *Austin Chronicle* restaurant poll, is Jeremiah's preferred dog, but the Abe Froman (a reference to *Ferris Bueller*) Chicago-style dog is his bestseller.

Originally from Bowie, Texas, Jeremiah grew up in Oklahoma. He was brought to Austin to celebrate his twenty-first birthday, and he instantly knew that the city was where he wanted to stay. Jeremiah states what Austinites love about our town: "Austin has all the big-city stuff in a small-city environment." He employs artists, waiters, and people seeking part-time work while they pursue other endeavors. His best suggestion for anyone wanting to get into the trailer food business is to "learn to be handy. I thought my first trailer on South First was a good deal, but I spent a bunch of money fixing it up. I know a lot more about trailer plumbing and wiring than I did before. It's good to fix things yourself if you're on a small budget."

Traditional Argentinian Empanada

Courtesy of mmmpanadas

Empanda \ pronounced
mmm-pah-NAH-dah /n:
vacation in your mouth.
Yield: 12 empanadas.

1 tablespoon olive oil
1 medium yellow onion,
chopped
2 tablespoons garlic, minced
1 pound lean ground beef
1 tablespoon fresh oregano,
finely chopped
2 teaspoons salt
2 teaspoons paprika
1 teaspoon cumin
1 cup tomato puree
½ cup sliced olives
1 package frozen puff pastry
dough
2 hard-boiled eggs, sliced
1 cup egg wash (4 beaten
eggs with 1 tablespoon
water and pinch of salt)

- Heat oil in a large saucepan. Add onion and soften. Once onion is translucent, add garlic and be ready to add beef. Once you smell the garlic, begin to add beef and brown.
- Mash beef to a fine texture. Add spices and tomato puree. Cook until liquid is evaporated. Remove mixture from heat, cool, and add olives.
- Roll out puff pastry dough. Use cookie cutter to cut 4-inch circles. Spoon 1 tablespoon of meat mixture onto each circle. Place 2 egg slices on top of each.
- Trace outer edges of dough circles with egg wash. Fold over front of empanada to create a half moon.
- Gently fork edges to seal empanada.
- With pastry brush, brush egg wash over all empanadas right before placing in a 350°F oven.
- Bake for 18 to 20 minutes. Cool on rack and enjoy!

mmmpanadas

Cody and Kristen Fields haphazardly fell into the empanada business in March of 2008. Prior to concocting delicious flavor pockets with a Tex-Mex flair, Cody was building wastewater treatment plants in Costa Rica. In Central America he discovered his love for eating empanadas, and a seed was planted. Upon his return to the States he met Kristen in Austin and decided he wanted to stay. While Cody was working the grind in a cube at a bank, he and Kristen began plotting his escape. As fate would have it, they stopped in at the Nomad, their neighborhood bar, one day before its grand opening. While the owner gave them a tour of the place, Kristen and Cody were joking around about empanadas. As if on cue, the bar owner shared that his empanada guy had fallen through. The next day, with little experience, they churned out about six-dozen empanadas. The bar owner loved the product and everything snowballed from there. Six months later they found a truck on eBay, bought it with a credit card, and they were in the empanada business.

Something that makes mmmpanadas unique from most other trailers in the Austin scene is that they promote their products, which are also currently available in grocery stores, with a roving trailer. The twenty-three-foot-long trailer is a moving billboard that also generates revenue. Cody's favorite item on the menu is also their bestseller: the Green Chile Chicken. Kristen's favorite is the Spicy Black Bean. They have a simple philosophy of making things the way they like to eat them, with four ingredients or fewer. Mmmpanadas has served the likes of Matthew McConaughey and members of Stone Temple Pilots, and the trailer is available for business lunches and festivals.

Tofu Scramble

Courtesy of Conscious Cravings

A light and warming vegetarian meal to share with a friend. Yield: serves 12.

16 ounces low-fat firm tofu
1 green bell pepper, chopped
1 cup chopped onions
1 teaspoon olive oil
1 tablespoon tamari
1 teaspoon Italian seasoning
1 teaspoon cumin
Black pepper to taste
Vegetable stock

- Drain the tofu and crumble into a bowl.
- Heat a large pan and add pepper, onions, olive oil, and tamari. Sauté for 3–4 minutes.
- Add the tofu, tamari, Italian seasoning, cumin, salt, pepper, and vegetable stock. Continue to sauté until heated through.

Conscious Cravings

Rishi Dhir spent four years on the Philly stock exchange before deciding to find a more laid-back career. As a vegetarian, he had created unique recipes based on his own dietary needs, and he thought he had something that might hold up with the general public. After checking out the Austin trailer food scene, he moved to the city and opened Conscious Cravings in August of 2010. Rishi's favorite dish is the Black Bean Slider Wrap.

A Day Trip to the Trailers: Southside

In the many pockets of trailer eateries on the buzzing streets of South Lamar, you can find farm-to-table dinners (Odd Duck Farm to Trailer), decadent oversized donuts (Gourdough's), Cuban food (The Texas Cuban), artisan cuisine (La Boîte), and more. On South Lamar, even the realtors work out of Airstreams. Tattoo shops, a lingerie shop next to a bar, tire dealers, window tint and collision businesses, psychics, and a new age book store all coexist within a few blocks.

Not far from South Lamar are the vendors of South 1st Street, selling tacos, cake balls, hot dogs, crepes, and much more. Taco connoisseurs will salivate over Torchy's "damn good tacos," located in a trailer oasis, the South Austin Trailer Park & Eatery. This park also hosts Holy Cacao (cake balls and cake shakes) and Man Bites Dog (hot dogs) under shady oak trees adorned with Christmas lights. In a game room backing up against Bouldin Creek, patrons can enjoy Ping-Pong, shuffleboard, and foosball, plus a beer or two, so long as they bring the beverages themselves.

On South 1st you'll also find neon signs, custom boot repair shops, and bridal boutiques. Where South 1st crosses Lady Bird Lake (formerly Town Lake), you'll find Auditorium Shores, a dog park right on the water's edge that sometimes turns into an outdoor music venue. Here you'll find the famous memorial statue of Stevie Ray Vaughn, local music legend. With it's lovely view of the downtown skyline, Auditorium Shores is a great place to bring your trailer food and watch what rolls by.

A hop, skip, and a jump from South Lamar and South 1st is Barton Springs Road. Running past Barton Springs, a natural spring-fed pool that Austinites enjoy with or without bikini tops, Barton Springs Road is home to several additional food trailers. And there are lots of fun things to do outside: have a picnic in Zilker Park, or take a stroll through the Zilker Botanical Garden and Umlauf Sculpture Garden.

Dinner

Royito's Wok Shrimp

Courtesy of Royito's Hot Sauce Streamer

Salsa meets the sea with this mouthwatering recipe. Yield: 2 servings.

1 pound fresh, medium shrimp, peeled and deveined (20-25 shrimp)
2 8-ounce jars Royito's Hot Sauce, divided
2 tablespoons olive oil
½ bell pepper (any color), chopped
½ white onion, chopped
Corn tortillas

- Marinate shrimp in 8 ounces of Royito's Hot Sauce for 2 hours in a sealed bowl.
- Heat olive oil in a large wok.
- Add pepper and onion and sauté for 4 minutes.
- Add shrimp and sauté for 4 minutes.
- Add a fresh 8 ounces of Royito's and let simmer an additional 5 minutes.
- Serve with warm corn tortillas and enjoy!

Quick and Easy Baby Back Ribs with Mustard BBQ Sauce

Courtesy of Smokilicious Bar-B-Q

Tailgating, BBQing at the lake, relaxing at the company picnic—there isn't a place that's not good for these eats.

3 to 4 racks baby back ribs

Boiling Liquid:
1 gallon water
1 cup apple cider vinegar
¼ cup Worcestershire sauce

Mustard BBQ Sauce:
½ cup yellow mustard
½ teaspoon Worcestershire sauce
⅓ cup apple cider vinegar
3 tablespoons dark brown sugar
¼ teaspoon salt
½ teaspoon pepper
¼ teaspoon cayenne pepper
½ teaspoon paprika
½ teaspoon mesquite seasoning (or hickory seasoning)

- Combine ribs and boiling liquid in a large pot and boil at a high, rapid boil for 30 to 40 minutes.
- While ribs are boiling, mix all sauce ingredients together in a small saucepan and let simmer for 5 to 10 minutes to allow all flavors to combine.
- Remove ribs from the liquid and place them bone-side down on a sheet pan. Pat dry with a paper towel and brush with sauce, covering both sides.
- Place ribs on a hot grill (indoor or outdoor), and cook to add a slight char and until sauce is caramelized, approximately 5 to 7 minutes on each side.

Eggplant Rollatini

Courtesy of Osmo's Kitchen

The Osmo's Kitchen trailer was developed out of Robin & Kent's love of culinary arts and has a dual-roots concept, offering a combination of Italian and Cajun cuisine. *A hint from the chef:* "I love cheese, so I sprinkle the top [of this dish] with mozzarella until it bubbles in the oven. Classically, this is only done with eggplant parmigiana—but you gotta have fun when you're the chef!"

Eggplant and Filling:

1 cup all-purpose flour
2 eggs, beaten
1 cup Italian bread crumbs
2 medium-size eggplants
1 cup olive oil and 1 cup vegetable oil for frying—you may need a little more
3 cups whole-milk ricotta cheese
1 cup Parmigiano-Reggiano cheese or good Parmesan
1 egg
2 tablespoons fresh Italian parsley, minced
6 fresh basil leaves, minced
Dried pepper flakes (optional)

Tomato Sauce:

½ cup olive oil (not extra-virgin)
1 medium onion, diced
1 carrot, diced
2 heaping tablespoons fresh garlic, minced
1 35-ounce can Italian whole tomatoes
8 good-size fresh basil leaves, divided
Kosher salt
Crushed red pepper to taste

For the eggplant and filling:
• Prepare your breading station with flour, eggs, and Italian bread crumbs.
• Slice off the stem and bottom of the eggplant. Remove the skin and slice eggplant lengthwise into ¼-inch slices. Set the slices on a paper towel. Bread each slice beginning with the flour first, the eggs second, and the bread crumbs last. Make sure you have a good coating on each slice, since otherwise the eggplant will absorb the oil very quickly.
• In a deep-set pan, heat olive oil mixed with the vegetable oil to 325°F. The sides of the eggplant should sizzle when placed into the oil. Fry slices to a golden brown on both sides. They will cook very quickly. After frying, place eggplant on paper towels to drain excess oil.
• Make the filling by mixing the ricotta and Parmigiano-Reggiano together in a mixing bowl. Beat the egg separately and then mix into the cheese mixture. Add minced Italian parsley and basil to the filling. Add dried pepper flakes if you like a little heat.

For the tomato sauce:
• Heat olive oil in a sauce pan. Add diced onion and sauté until onion is lightly browned. Add diced carrot and continue to cook on lower heat until carrot is softened, then add minced garlic. With clean hands, crush the Italian whole tomatoes and add to the pot along with the juice and one basil leaf. Add kosher salt and crushed red pepper to taste. Bring to a boil and reduce to a simmer for about 45 minutes. After 45 minutes, add remaining basil leaves and let them steep in the sauce.

To assemble:
• Prepare a 13- by 9-inch baking dish with enough tomato sauce to cover the bottom, just thick enough so the eggplant doesn't burn. Place 2 tablespoons of filling on one end of each eggplant slice and roll them, placing the seam side down into the baking dish. Coat the eggplant with the tomato sauce and sprinkle grated cheese on top of the rollatini and bake, covered, in a 350°F degree oven for 25 to 35 minutes.

The Flying Carpet

Maria and Abderrahim Souktouri are the heart and soul of The Flying Carpet and grew up in cultures as bold and brilliant as the food they serve. Maria grew up in Austin, while Abderrahim hales from a ghetto in Morocco. He won his United States citizenship in the lottery when he was twenty-seven. They met at a party for the Latin American Studies department at UT and ended up hooking up at Club Rio. Eventually they married and had their first-born, Talib, and with his birth came a change in lifestyle. With a leap of faith, Maria quit her job as a paralegal for a civil rights attorney in order to stay home with Talib while Abderrahim kept his job at the Dell factory. During this time of chance, the couple decided to do something "just for them" and try their hand at the food industry.

Maria tells it like this: "We've always entertained and been foodies; having parties for thirty to forty people at our house is not a strange thing. People rant and rave about our food and we'd talked about what it would be like to open a restaurant ever since we first got together fifteen years ago. But we knew enough to be scared. When we thought about opening the trailer we also came up with plans B and C. Plan B was to sell the trailer. Plan C was to move to Morocco. But there were so many confirmations once we started the business, and I realized that the house, the biggest thing we'll ever buy, even if we lose it, doesn't change who we are. Life isn't a dress rehearsal; it's now. What are we waiting for? The trailer was something we could financially and logistically do."

Abderrahim first tested the waters with his trailer food endeavors in Morocco. He had a street-food business there, selling roasted nuts. He has taken his bride to his hometown twice, and his son has been once so far. The couple feels strongly about serving people what they would eat out of their own home, so all of the ingredients come from hormone-free and cage-free animals and they use organic vegetables. Former Barton Springs lifeguard Maria says, "The food in Morocco is clean and brilliant because it is not mass-produced. Even though I'm Mexican, we never ate at trailers because they were dirty. But Morocco is different."

In fact, The Moroccan wrap is the Souktouri's bestseller. For this dish, they use a pure bread made of flour, salt, and water that they buy daily. Next, they pour on a tomato sauce that includes peeled tomatoes that have been slow-cooked in spices, onions, and garlic. (The sauce cooks for at least two and a half hours.) They then plop three little nuggets of vegetarian-fed, hormone-free beef on top. A vegetarian-fed, hormone-free, cage-free fried egg is added as a final touch. If that doesn't have your taste buds watering for underground soul food, I don't know what else to write.

Moroccan Lemon Butter and Olive Chicken with French Fries

Courtesy of The Flying Carpet

This dish is one of the Souktori family's favorites, and soon will be one of yours, too. This chicken is often served with a cucumber/tomato salad, French fries, and bread to sop up the sauce.

Chicken and Fries:
1 large whole chicken, washed and dried, skin on
1½ cups green olives (no brine)
Skinny French fries

Paste:
½ cup olive oil
1 stalk cilantro, finely chopped
1 medium onion, finely chopped
3 small garlic cloves, finely chopped
½ teaspoon ginger
2 teaspoons paprika
1 teaspoon cumin
½ teaspoon turmeric
2 teaspoons fine sea salt
1 teaspoon coarse black pepper
Juice of one medium-large lemon; reserve halves
½ stick salted butter, slightly softened

- Mix the paste ingredients together.
- Cover chicken with paste outside and inside the skin.
- Insert lemon halves used for their juice inside the chicken.
- Cook at 350°F for 1½ hours or until done. Every 20 or 30 minutes, baste chicken in its own juices with a spoon or baster.
- Add green olives to the chicken for the last 10 to 15 minutes of cooking time. The olives will fall to the sides and into the chicken's juices—this is what you want.
- Make French fries according to package instructions to have hot and ready at the same time chicken is finishing.
- Serve a slice of chicken atop the French fries and pour sauce with olives from pan liberally on top of the entire dish.

Crawfish Étouffée

Courtesy of Turf N Surf Po' Boy

Creator of his rustic Turf N Surf trailer, chef Ralph Gilmore also designed this étouffée. Yield: 8 servings.

- In a saucepan, sauté the following:
  - 1 stick organic butter
  - ½ red bell pepper, chopped
  - ½ sweet white onion, chopped
  - 4 carrots, chopped
  - 3 garlic cloves, minced
  - 3 celery sticks, chopped

- Make a roux with the above by adding a little flour, browning to your taste, and adding:
  - 1½ teaspoon paprika
  - 1½ teaspoon Old Bay seasoning
  - 1 teaspoon crushed red pepper
  - 1 teaspoon thyme
  - 2 bay leaves
  - Pepper to taste
  - 1 teaspoon chicken base
  - Juice of 3 lemons

- Add water to achieve the consistency of a gravy.
- Add 2 pounds crawfish tails and cook until done.
- Serve on a toasted po' boy bun.
- Dress to impress with lettuce, tomato, coleslaw, onions, and pickle slices.

Turf N Surf Po' Boy

"I liked cooking before cooking was cool," states Ralph Gilmore of Turf N Surf Po' Boy. Ralph brings his background not only in the restaurant industry but also his experience designing and building custom homes and choppers to the table as the designer and chef of his trailer that is currently located downtown. After buying the most raw and rustic unit he could find, he began molding the cart with a turf-and-surf feel. The majority of the items that make up his décor are recycled and he used less than 5 percent wood in his build-out. Continuing with the overall green feel of his food trailer, Ralph buys his produce locally. "I just wanted to do something that gives back to the people," he explains about his choice to buy from Austin-area farmers.

Ralph is most proud of his fried shrimp, and it's also his bestseller. Having opened in April of 2010, he has some advice for new vendors: "Watch out for August. The heat factor, getting back to school, and last-minute vacations put you in the hole if you don't have the capitol to get through it. But if it's your dream, stay with it."

East Side King

Business partners Moto and Paul developed the famed East Side King trailer concept of "Good South Asian Street Food" because they felt this cuisine was lacking in the Austin area. Hailing from a small island in southern Japan, Moto has been in Austin for twenty years. The trailer is eponymously named after his blues and soul band. The Thai Chicken Karaage is not only the owner's favorite, it is also his bestseller.

Thai Chicken Karaage

Courtesy of East Side King

The famed East Side King trailer concept of "Good South Asian Street Food" was developed by business partners Moto and Paul. The trailer's name comes from Moto's blues and soul band, which has the same title. The Chicken Karaage is a bestseller and Moto's personal favorite item on the menu.

3 pounds chicken legs, boned and cut into large bite-size chunks
2 cups cornstarch
4 cups vegetable oil
4 ounces white onion, sliced thinly
2 ounces jalapeño, sliced into thin rounds
3 ounces cilantro, picked and washed
1½ ounces mint, picked and washed
1½ ounce Thai basil, picked and washed
8 ounces Thai Chicken Sauce (recipe below)

Thai Chicken Sauce:
4 ounces water
4 ounces white vinegar
4 ounces white sugar
1 ounces sweet chili sauce (see recipe below)
2 ounces fish sauce
1½ ounces garlic
1½ ounces Thai chili, minced

Combine in a bowl and whisk until all ingredients are fully incorporated.

Sweet Chili Sauce:
4 ounces white vinegar
2 ounces white sugar
1 ounces chili flakes

In a small sauce pot, combine the vinegar and sugar. Allow the mixture to come to a boil without stirring. Add the chili flakes and stir.

Chicken Karaage:
• Lightly toss the cut chicken in the cornstarch, until each piece is evenly coated and there are no moist spots. Preheat oil to 375°F.
• Fry chicken until golden brown and cooked throughout.
• Move the hot chicken to a large bowl, add the onions, jalapeño, and herbs, and then add the sauce. Toss gently, and be sure to coat all pieces with a good amount of sauce. Transfer to a serving dish and enjoy!

Dirty Water Dog

Courtesy of Big Top Dogs

Authentic New York–style hot dogs.

2 all-beef, natural-casing Sabrett hot dogs
1¼ stick of butter
1 ounce of Sabrett pushcart style mustard
2 ounces Sabrett sauerkraut
1 ounce Sabrett Onions in Sauce (Vidalia onions that have been cooked in a tomato and vinegar sauce. If you cannot find this, see recipe on page 76)
1 Coney bun with sesame seeds (such as Rainbow brand)

• Cut open one hot dog and let simmer in a pot of water and butter for about an hour. This will impart some of the hot dog's au jus into the water and enhance flavor of the additional dogs you are going to cook.
• Simmer sauerkraut in a pan for about 15 minutes.
• Simmer Onions in Sauce in another pan for 15 minutes.
• Bring hot dog water up to full boil and add the hot dog.
• Spread a dollop of mustard on the bun. When hot dog is plump and floating in water, remove and place on bun.
• Top with sauerkraut.
• Top the sauerkraut with a small line of Onions in Sauce.

Rotisserie Chicken

Courtesy of The Jalopy

This rotisserie chicken from The Jalopy stands alone, but it also can be shredded to use in sandwiches and other creations.

4- to 5-pound whole chicken
1 gallon water
2 cups sea salt
½ cup honey (molasses works as well)
½ cup soy sauce
A few sprigs of thyme
A tuft of rosemary
1 part black pepper
1 part white pepper
1 part coriander
1 part cayenne pepper
5 parts kosher salt
Melted butter

- Brine chicken overnight in a gallon of water with the sea salt, honey, soy sauce, thyme, and rosemary.
- Dab the chicken dry and coat liberally with the combined seasonings: black and white pepper, coriander, cayenne, and kosher salt.
- Rotisserie (broil) chicken on high (375–450°F) for 10 minutes. Brush the chicken with butter (this gives it that golden sheen).
- Turn heat down on the rotisserie to about 245–260°F for 70 to 80 minutes.
- Let cool for 10 to 15 minutes, then voilà . . . the perfect rotisserie chicken.

Fajita Quesadilla with Cilantro Cream Sauce

Courtesy of Colibri Cuisine

Authentic Mexican-American cuisine meets the streets. Yield: 4 servings.

½ pound top sirloin skirt steak
½ cup yellow onions, fajita cut
1 large serrano pepper
1 medium green bell pepper
1 medium red bell pepper
4 10-inch flour tortillas
2 cups Monterey Jack cheese
1 large tomato, diced
Kosher salt to taste
Freshly ground black
  peppercorns to taste

Cilantro Cream Sauce:
1 bunch cilantro leaves,
  chopped (no stems)
½ cup green onion tops,
  chopped
6 ounces sour cream
1½ ounces lime juice

- Mix chopped cilantro and green onions with sour cream and add lime juice to taste. Add salt if desired.
- Grill seasoned steak on griddle to proper temperature.
- Sauté onions; julienne all peppers and sauté.
- Heat tortillas until warm.
- Top with cheese to cover tortilla. Add steak, onions, peppers, and diced tomatoes. Season with salt and pepper to taste.

Colibri Cuisine

Since he was five years old, Anthony remembers begging his grandparents to buy him a special food trailer just like the one that was next door to them. So after quitting his accounting job and attempting a career in teaching, Anthony had a life realization. "I kept telling my students 'Follow your dreams, you can be whatever you want to be, stick with it,'" and I felt like a hypocrite because I never pursued my own dreams of owning a trailer food business. Then, I finally made a decision to do what I always wanted to do." So he moved to Austin to go to culinary school at Le Cordon Bleu, and he has been operating his trailer since October of 2009. He is the first of his family to graduate from college, and his grandmother and mother have both visited him at Colibri with proud hearts for all he has accomplished.

Moroccan Fish with Vegetables

Courtesy of The Flying Carpet

An exotic and healthy feast from the shores of Morocco. Yield: 4 servings.

5 tablespoons olive oil
1 medium bunch of cilantro, finely chopped
1 medium onion, finely chopped
Juice of 1 large lemon
½ teaspoon salt
1 teaspoon paprika (smoky not sweet)
½ teaspoon turmeric
¼ teaspoon black pepper
¼ teaspoon ground ginger
¼ teaspoon cumin
3 medium potatoes, peeled and cut into medium/thin rounds
1 large green bell pepper, diced large
3 large carrots, peeled; cut whole carrot into 3 sections and then cut each piece in half lengthwise
2 medium tomatoes, peeled, diced small
1 whole jalapeño
1 whole large lemon, cut into rounds, seeds removed
4 6-ounce portions salmon or tuna fillets
1 cup large green olives (with pimiento, stuffed with jalapeño, or plain)

- In a large bowl, mix olive oil, cilantro, onions, lemon juice, and spices. Add vegetables, whole jalapeño, and lemon rounds; stir well.
- Pour half of the mixture into a glass baking dish, then add fish fillets, finally topping with remainder of vegetable/spice mixture.
- Bake at 350°F until carrots and potatoes are almost soft; add olives and cook until carrots and potatoes are completely done (5 to 10 minutes more). Serve with sliced, fresh-baked baguette.

Kebabalicious

Midway through their first semester of college, business partners Chris and Christian took off for an opportunity to snowboard and work at a hotel in Switzerland. Although they wouldn't be able to leave work very often, the guys took advantage of the Swiss live music scene when they could and subsequently would hit up a local food trailer called Kebab 2001, which was where the Kebabalicious trailer story starts.

A Turkish entrepreneur in Switzerland, Demir, took Chris under his wing and gave him an opportunity to go into his big facility to learn how cook Turkish food. Chris says, "Without him, I wouldn't know how to do it. He liked me, but I had to push to open the door and work with fifty-two Turkish guys. I had to do some smooth talking to get in. Without that I wouldn't know how to do any of the sauces." Demir had started out twenty years prior with a little stand, and it took him ten years to expand enough to get out of the kebab stand scene. He is now running a million pounds of beef and lamb per week through his factory. Demir told Chris, "I can't pay you but I like that you want to take this back to Texas. You can't ever come back to Switzerland and open a kebab stand and put me out of business."

Spinach and Feta Böreks

Courtesy of Kebabalicious

Hailed as the best böreks in the U.S. by many a European traveler, these savory pastries are sure to please any guest you serve. Yield: 24 triangular böreks.

Spinach Filling:
3½ pounds fresh organic spinach
¼ cup extra-virgin olive oil
2 tablespoons clarified organic butter
7 red Fresno peppers, seeds removed, and diced
1 cup shallots, minced
½ cup organic red onion, minced
½ cup fresh garlic, minced
Peruvian pink salt and fresh-ground Tellicherry peppercorns to taste
3 farm-fresh eggs
2 cups crumbled sheep's milk feta
½ cup fresh organic Italian parsley, minced

Pastry:
1 farm fresh-egg
¼ cup 2% organic milk
3 tablespoons olive oil
¼ cup organic butter, melted
1 pound phyllo dough

Glaze:
2 tablespoons pure honey
½ cup 2% organic milk
3 farm-fresh eggs

4 tablespoons melted organic butter

For Filling:
- Pre-heat oven to 400°F.
- Blanch the spinach in boiling water for 2 minutes, until tender—don't overcook.
- Cool in ice water, then pat/squeeze dry. In a skillet, heat olive oil and clarified butter, then sauté peppers, shallots, and onions for 5 minutes over medium heat, stirring frequently. Next, add garlic and continue to sauté until garlic is light brown. Add chopped, cool/dry spinach to pan and stir together for 2 to 3 minutes. Add salt and pepper to taste. Last but not least, when mix has cooled, add eggs, feta, and parsley to the spinach concoction and stir. Place in fridge while prepping pastry.

For Pastry:
- Place egg, milk, olive oil, and butter in a bowl and whisk together. Brush this mixture on a rectangular deep-dish baking pan. Now unroll phyllo dough (make sure dough is at room temperature) and place one sheet on pan. Brush the dough with a very light layer of butter mixture.

Place another sheet of phyllo dough on top of the first and brush with butter mixture. Continue to repeat this step and layer about 8 to 10 sheets of buttered-up phyllo back-to-back. Don't let the other sheets of phyllo dough dry out while working—cover them.
- Once this bottom phyllo dough foundation is completed in the deep-dish pan, take the cooled spinach mix and spread it over the foundation phyllo. Use all the spinach mix. Now cover with another sheet of phyllo dough to create the top crust and brush it with the butter mixture. Use the same technique you used to create the bottom phyllo foundation for the top phyllo crust, layering 8 to 10 sheets.
- Whisk the glaze ingredients together. Brush the glaze over the final top phyllo layer for a golden-brown finish! We recommend cutting or scoring the börek into triangular pieces before cooking. Bake for 16 to 18 minutes, then lower heat to 350°F and bake for another 18 minutes (granted, all ovens have their quirks). When the böreks are golden-brown, remove from oven and let them cool for a few minutes before serving.

Meatballs in Marinara

Courtesy of All-City Subs

A classic dish that is good year-round and even better the next day. Yield: 6–8 servings.

Meatballs:
Small red onion
Green bell pepper
3 to 4 gloves of garlic
3 links sweet Italian sausage
1 pound 80/20 ground beef
1 egg
⅓ cup bread crumbs
1 tablespoon basil
1 tablespoon parsley
1 tablespoon crushed red pepper
1 tablespoon oregano
Dash of rosemary
Dash of sage
Dash of thyme
Dash of kosher salt

- Preheat oven to 325°F.
- Chop and blend onion, pepper, and garlic together.
- Remove sausage from casings and crumble.
- Using only half of the blended onion/pepper/garlic combo, add all ingredients together in a mixing bowl. Using your hands, mix all ingredients thoroughly.
- Roll into 2.5-ounce, tightly packed balls and place on a baking sheet. Place in the oven for 20 to 25 minutes (or until internal temperature is 125°).
- Remove the meatballs from the oven; gently place them on a plate with paper towel to absorb the grease. Cool the meatballs so they do not fall apart when stirred into the sauce.
- Once the meatballs have cooled, gently place them into the sauce and continue to gently stir.
- Continue to slow cook and stir the sauce for approximately 30 minutes, or until meatballs reach an internal temperature of 160°F.

Marinara:
2 cans (28 ounces each) crushed tomatoes
1 small can of tomato paste
The remaining half of the onion/pepper/garlic combo
½ bottle of white cooking wine
2 tablespoons sugar
2 tablespoons basil

- Over low heat, in a large pot, slowly mix all ingredients together one at a time. Continuously stir the sauce while it cooks to prevent sticking and burning. This is a basic marinara.
- Note: if cooking pasta to add to this dish, make sure you cook the pasta al dente; then, add it to the sauce as well and let it cook the rest of the way in the sauce.

86 This! Green Chili Chicken Enchiladas

Courtesy of 86 This

Can't beat these with a stick. Yield: 6–8 enchiladas.

6 cups chicken broth
3 4-ounce cans diced Hatch green chiles (mild or hot your choice), divided
2 cups chopped yellow onion, divided
6 tablespoons ground cumin, divided
1 regular-size chicken (Think Goldilocks—not too big, not too small)
10 6-inch corn tortillas
4 cloves garlic, minced
1 tablespoons black pepper
4 tablespoons butter
3 tablespoons flour
1 8-ounce container sour cream
2 cups shredded Monterey Jack cheese, divided
1 cup chopped roma tomatoes
1 bunch chopped green onions

- Put chicken broth in large stockpot with 1 can diced chiles, 1 cup chopped onion, and 3 tablespoons cumin. Place chicken in pot. Add water to cover by at least 2 inches. Boil until done.
- Remove chicken and set aside. Reserve stock. When chicken is cool, remove meat from bone and set aside.
- Heat oven to 350°F. Wrap the tortillas in foil and bake them for about 10 minutes, or wrap in paper towels and nuke them for 2 minutes until they're soft.
- In a saucepan, sauté remaining onions, garlic, remaining cumin, and pepper in butter until onions are tender. In a separate bowl, combine flour and sour cream, then add to onion mixture with the remaining cans of chiles.

Cook and stir continuously until thickened and bubbly.
- Remove from heat, and stir in 1 cup of the cheese.
- Put 1 cup of the sauce in the shredded chicken and mix it up so it's gooey. Put about ⅓ cup of chicken filling into each tortilla and wrap it up. Then put them in a casserole dish.
- Pour the rest of the sauce over the enchiladas, then cover with foil. Bake at 350°F for 35 minutes. Then remove the foil and sprinkle the remaining 1 cup of cheese over the top.
- Bake uncovered for about 5 minutes more, or until the cheese is melted. When ready to serve, sprinkle the top with the tomatoes and green onions.

86 This

Business partners Michelle Patronella and Mark Bradford realized they had a similar love for the hustle and bustle of the food industry when they met working at a local Tex-Mex restaurant. One of their personal favorite items on the menu is the Multi-tasker, a variation on Mark's mother's recipe for a roasted brisket and mashed potato sandwich. The pair is very positive about the trailer food movement in Austin. "Seeing a new trailer makes us happy, even if it's a halfhearted attempt. People shouldn't be scared to follow their dreams."

Pierogies

Courtesy of Trey's Cuisine

Multicultural, delectable dumplings. Yield: 30 pierogies.

Pasta Dough:
9 eggs
6 cups flour
2 tablespoons olive/canola oil blend
1 tablespoon salt

Mix:
6 Russet potatoes
½ cup shredded Monterey Jack
½ cup shredded Swiss
½ cup shredded cheddar
¼ cup shredded Asiago
Salt to taste

Cornmeal:
4 to 6 cups vegetable oil

- Prep pasta: Blend all ingredients in a stand mixer until dough is formed. Chill.
- Prep mix: Boil potatoes and mash hot with all shredded cheeses. Chill.
- Prep pierogies: Roll dough to ⅛-inch thickness. Cut into 1 by 1-inch squares, or size of your liking.
- Place 1½ ounces of potato mixture on dough. Roll in a cylinder and crimp edges. Dust with cornmeal for storage.
- To cook: Heat fryer to 375°F. Cook in oil for 3 to 5 minutes, until golden brown.

Trey's Cuisine

Cowden Ward has more than twenty years of experience in the food world, and he has served such celebrities as Clint Eastwood, Billy Joel, and Ann Richards. He opened Pick Up Stix, his first concession trailer venture, upon returning from Europe. Since then, he has re-opened as Trey's Cuisine with a new concept and an expanded menu featuring some of his favorite dishes from the Mediterranean and Northern Europe. His personal favorite item on the menu is the Greek Chicken Croquette, which is a chicken, rice, cream cheese, artichoke, spinach, and feta patty fried and served on a bed of lettuce or rice.

Parts of his culinary endeavors were inspired by both of his grandmothers' cookbooks, as well as his mother, who was from French Louisiana. Outside of her gumbo, Cowden says his mom's best recipe was a chicken curry dish served cold with white rice and green onions. He hopes to one day learn how to fly in order to expedite getting fresh soft-shell crab on his menu. For now, patrons can enjoy a worldly menu of croquette sliders, kebabs, and perogies.

Sweets

Fredericksburg Peach-Blackberry Pie

Courtesy of Cutie Pies

> Fresh summertime peaches and blackberries that make their way to this pie will put the "doo-dah back in your zip-a-dee!"

Crust:

1 cup flour
½ cup Crisco butter
¼ cup ice water

Place flour and shortening in bowl and mix together until it forms small balls about the size of peas. Add your ice water. It is very important to place your water in the freezer just until ice chips form on the top of the water, then add to your flour mixture. This makes for a wet dough, but keep working it into a ball and wrap in plastic wrap and refrigerate for at least 30 minutes. Roll out as normal for a 9-inch pie.

Filling:

¼ cup brown sugar
¼ cup butter
¼ cup lime juice
3 tablespoons cornstarch
3 cups fresh peaches, sliced
1 cup fresh blackberries
¼ teaspoon ground cloves
¼ teaspoon ground nutmeg
½ teaspoon ground cinnamon

Place sugar, butter, lime juice, and cornstarch in small container and microwave until melted; stir well. Place peach slices in bowl, add blackberries and spices, then add your melted roux. Mix well. Pour into pie shell and add several dots of butter. At this point you may either do a typical lattice crust or crumb topping. Bake at 350°F for 30 to 40 minutes.

Cutie Pies

Jaynie Buckingham is rightfully the self-proclaimed Pie Queen of Austin, Texas. For the eight years prior to opening Cutie Pies, Jaynie was a hospice nurse. Her leap from bedpans to pie pans came when her buttermilk pie won a contest at the historic Driskill hotel downtown. The pie is now featured on the menu at the Driskill. Her same pie recipe has been highlighted in Martha Stewart's *Living* magazine and was awarded "Best Pie in the South" by *Southern Living* magazine. Although Buttermilk Pie is her signature dessert, her personal favorite on the menu is the White Chocolate Coconut Pecan. Those two along with her Dutch Chocolate Pie are her top three sellers. "Come on down to the pie wagon where you can stuff your pie hole because my pies will put the doo-dah back in your zip-a-dee," Jaynie says.

Fullilove Hershey Pie

Courtesy of Cutie Pies

Wondering about the title of this treat? This is the Pie Queen's Aunt Tommie's recipe, and her last name was Fullilove!

1 package Graham Crackers
Dash of cinnamon
8-ounce Hershey bar with
  or without almonds (your
  preference)
⅓ cup milk
25 marshmallows
1 8-ounce container Cool Whip
Whipped cream
Chocolate shavings

- Prepare graham cracker crust according to package directions, adding cinnamon.
- Melt Hershey bar and milk over double boiler or in microwave until smooth. Add marshmallows to mix until all are melted. Let cool to room temperature.
- Put Cool Whip in a large bowl and add chocolate mixture. Fold in gently until mixed well. Pour into pie shell and chill for at least 2 hours to give it time to set.
- Garnish with whipped cream and chocolate shavings.

Red Velvet Cake Balls with Cream Cheese Frosting

Courtesy of Holy Cacao

Holy Cacao makes red velvet cake and cream cheese frosting from scratch with fresh ingredients, as described in the recipes below. Then, they dip the cake balls in a special couverture chocolate available through baking suppliers. However, when they were learning to make cake balls, they practiced with Duncan Hines red velvet cake mix, cream cheese frosting, and Wilton's candy melts; these ingredients work fine for making your own cake balls at home.

Cake:

¾ cup unsalted butter, softened
2 cups sugar
3 large eggs, at room temperature
3 tablespoons red food paste
3 tablespoons cocoa powder
1¾ teaspoons Madagascar vanilla bean paste
1½ teaspoon salt
3½ cups cake flour
1½ cups buttermilk
1½ teaspoons white vinegar
1½ teaspoons baking soda

- Preheat oven to 350°F. Grease a 13-by-9-inch pan.
- In a large bowl, on the medium speed of an electric mixer, cream the butter and sugar until light and fluffy (about 5 minutes). Add the eggs, one at a time, beating well after each addition. In a small bowl, whisk together the food paste, cocoa, vanilla paste, and salt. Add to the batter and beat well.
- Sift cake flour into a small bowl. Alternately add cake flour and buttermilk to batter. Stir together the vinegar and baking soda and add it to the batter as well.
- Pour the batter into the pan and bake for 30 to 35 minutes, or until a tester inserted into the cake comes out clean.

Cream Cheese Frosting:

1 cup cream cheese, softened
⅓ cup powdered sugar, sifted
1½ tablespoons lemon juice

- Process softened cream cheese in a food processor until smooth. Add powdered sugar and lemon juice and beat until smooth.

Cake Balls:

- Now the fun and messy part begins! Clean your hands well and dig in. Once the cake has cooled completely, crumble it into a large bowl. (Set aside a couple handfuls of cake crumbs to return to the oven and toast for cake ball topping.) Add frosting, 1 tablespoon at a time, and press it into the cake crumbs until a mud consistency is reached (there will be frosting left over). Chill the mixture in the refrigerator for 1 hour or longer.
- To make the balls, use a small #40 scooper or tablespoon to measure a cake mixture amount. Roll the cake mixture into balls and place them on a cookie sheet lined with parchment paper. Once all the mixture has been rolled, place the balls in the freezer for at least 1 hour.
- Melt Wilton's Chocolate Melts (white, dark, or milk chocolate) in microwave according to package directions. Dip Popsicle sticks halfway into the melted chocolate and then stick them into the cake balls. Return the balls to the freezer for a few minutes, then submerge the entire ball into the melted chocolate, and then shake off excess chocolate. Sit the ball into the toasted cake crumbs or sugar crystals. After the chocolate has dried, the cake balls are ready to serve.

Chocolate Brioche Bread Pudding with Cherry-Bourbon Sauce

Courtesy of La Boîte

"When the café first opened, brioches were not well known, and frequently we'd find ourselves with some of these delightful individual chocolate-filled breads left at the end of the day. We saved a few days' worth and then made this bread pudding for friends over the holidays. It was sublime!" — Victoria Davies, owner, La Boîte. Yield: 6–8 servings.

For the Pudding:

8 chocolate-filled brioches
8 large eggs
¾ cup sugar
4 cups whole milk
1½ teaspoons vanilla
½ teaspoon salt

1. Preheat oven to 350°F.

2. Cut/break the brioches into pieces about 1½ inches wide.

3. Place brioche pieces on a baking sheet and place in the oven until lightly toasted. Remove from oven and allow to cool.

4. To make custard mix, beat eggs until thick and add sugar, milk, vanilla, and salt. Mix until thoroughly blended.

5. Put brioche pieces into a buttered 8-by-8-inch baking dish and pour the custard mix over. Let sit for approximately 10 minutes and add any remaining custard.

6. Cover the dish with foil and bake for approximately an hour, or until the liquid custard has cooked.

7. Remove pudding and allow to sit for 10 minutes prior to serving.

For the Cherry-Bourbon Sauce:

½ cup butter
1 bag of frozen organic pitted sour cherries
1 cup sugar
1 egg, lightly beaten
2 to 3 tablespoons bourbon

1. Combine butter, sugar, and egg in small saucepan and cook over low heat, whisking constantly, until mixture thickens; do not boil.

2. Stir in cherries and allow to cook for another 5 minutes, ensuring the mixture doesn't boil.

3. Remove from heat and stir in bourbon.

Moroccan Lemon Kisses

Courtesy of The Flying Carpet

From Morocco with love.
Yield: approximately 50 small
cookies, or 25 larger cookies.

1½ sticks butter (room
   temperature)
1¼ cup sugar
1 egg (room temperature)
1 egg yolk (room temperature)
1 teaspoon Mexican vanilla
2 tablespoons lemon juice (must
   be fresh and room temperature)
Rind of three large lemons
¼ teaspoon salt
½ teaspoon baking powder
2½ cups flour

- In a bowl, cream butter, sugar,
  eggs, vanilla, lemon juice,
  and rind. In a separate bowl,
  mix salt, baking powder, and
  flour. Slowly incorporate dry
  ingredients with wet.
- Transfer dough to a work
  surface. Shape into 2 disks,
  cover with plastic wrap, and
  refrigerate for at least 1 hour
  or up to 3 days.
- Preheat oven to 350°F.
- On a lightly floured work
  surface, roll out dough to
  ⅛-inch thickness. Cut into
  desired shapes, and transfer
  to prepared baking sheets,
  leaving an inch in between
  each cookie. Leftover
  dough can be rolled and
  cut once more. Bake until
  lightly golden, about 10 to
  12 minutes; do not allow to
  brown.

Put-Your-Fork-into-It Cheesecake

Courtesy of Lil' Mama's Delicious Desserts 'n More

Once you start eating this cheesecake, you won't be able to stop. Yield: 8–16 servings (depending on how big the slices are cut).

Crust:
1½ cups graham cracker crumbs
¼ cup sugar
⅓ cup butter or margarine, melted

Cheesecake Batter:
3 8-ounce packages cream cheese, softened
1 cup sugar
1 teaspoon vanilla
4 eggs

- Preheat oven to 325°F.
- Mix graham crumbs, ¼ cup sugar, and butter; press onto bottom of 9-inch springform pan.
- Beat cream cheese, 1 cup sugar, and vanilla with mixer until well blended. Add eggs, one at a time, mixing on low speed after each, just until blended. Pour over crust.
- Bake 55 minutes or until center is almost set.
- Place cheesecake in refrigerator for at least 4 hours.
- Once chilled, take the back side of a knife (non-bladed edge) and slowly and carefully run it around the inside edge of the pan and cheesecake to loosen. Then unlock the latch of the springform pan and remove.
- Top as desired or serve plain.

Lil' Mama's Delicious Desserts 'n More

Heather Biagas started baking when she was thirteen years old. She grew up in Boston, where she spent some time getting to know the restaurant business by waiting tables, and she has precious memories of making pound cake while visiting her grandmother in Trinidad. She also completed an internship baking cakes for Disney World while earning her culinary degree. While the biggest takeaway was her lessons in customer service, the most interesting cake she baked for Disney was a checkerboard cake with vanilla and chocolate pieces and multiple tiers.

Heather's personal favorite item on the menu is the cheesecake. "That [cheesecake] is what got me interested in baking. I would go to restaurants and notice [their cheesecakes] were really tall. I wondered how they could still be so good. I love cheesecake because you can add anything to it. Whether it's fudge swirl or strawberry, everything is good with cheesecake." She loves the flexibility and creativity involved in baking. About her grandmother's pound cake, she says, "You can dress it up, like with a berry parfait, or you can dress it down and make it like a biscuit. That is the reason my husband married me, because I can make a good pound cake."

Lil' Mama's food trailer began in May 2008. The company had been a dream since she was in middle school. She has extensively researched and tested her recipes, and everything is baked with love.

Grandma's Classic Pound Cake

Courtesy of Lil' Mama's Delicious Desserts 'n More

Eat this classic cake by itself or top with ice cream and strawberries.

3 cups all-purpose flour
1 tablespoon coarse salt
3 sticks softened unsalted butter, plus more for pans
2 cups sugar
1 teaspoon pure vanilla extract
6 large eggs, at room temperature

- Preheat oven to 325°F. Butter two 5-by-9-inch loaf pans. Combine all-purpose flour and salt in a bowl.
- Cream butter and sugar with a mixer on high speed until pale and fluffy (about 8 minutes).

Scrape down sides of bowl. Reduce speed to medium, and add vanilla extract.

- Lightly beat eggs, and add to mixer bowl in 4 additions, mixing thoroughly after each and scraping down sides. Reduce speed to low, and add flour mixture in 4 additions, mixing until just incorporated. Divide batter between pans. Tap on counter to distribute; smooth tops.
- Bake until a tester inserted into center of each cake comes out clean (about 65 minutes). Let cool in pans on a wire rack for 30 minutes. Remove from pans and let cool completely on wire rack.

Brownies

Courtesy of Little Bean Bakery & Café

The chocolate chunk pieces are critical to achieving brownie perfection.

4 large eggs
1 cup sugar
1 cup brown sugar
8 ounces butter, melted
2 teaspoons vanilla extract
1¼ cups cocoa powder, sifted
½ cup flour, sifted
½ teaspoon salt
Chocolate chunk pieces
Hershey's Double Chocolate
  Sundae Syrup

- Preheat oven to 300°F and grease an 8-by-8-inch pan.
- Whisk eggs until fluffy and light in color.
- Add both sugars and mix well.
- Add the butter and vanilla.
- Sift in the cocoa powder, flour, and salt and mix well.
- Stir in chocolate chunks.
- Pour mixture into pan and smooth out. Drizzle chocolate syrup over the top and swirl with a knife. Bake for 45 minutes.

Brown Butter with Candied-Bacon Ice Cream

Courtesy of Coolhaus

Serve between homemade chocolate chip cookies for a delicious ice cream sandwich.

5 strips bacon
2 tablespoons light brown sugar

Brown Butter Ice Cream:
3 tablespoons salted butter
¾ cup brown sugar
2¾ cups half-and-half, divided
5 large egg yolks
2 teaspoons dark rum or whiskey
¼ teaspoon vanilla extract
¼ teaspoon ground cinnamon
(optional)

Candied Bacon:
- Preheat oven to 400°F.
- Lay the strips of bacon on a baking sheet lined with aluminum foil, shiny side down.
- Sprinkle 1½ to 2 teaspoons of brown sugar evenly over each strip of bacon.
- Bake for 12 to 16 minutes. Midway during baking, flip the bacon strips over and drag them through the dark, syrupy liquid that's collected on the baking sheet. Continue to bake until deep brown. Remove from oven and cool the strips on a rack.
- Once crisp and cool, chop into little pieces.

Brown Butter Ice Cream:
- Melt the butter in a heavy, medium-size saucepan. Stir in the brown sugar and half of the half-and-half.
- In a separate bowl, stir together the egg yolks, then gradually add some of the warm brown sugar mixture to them, whisking the yolks constantly as you pour. Pour the mixture back into the saucepan. Cook over low to moderate heat, constantly stirring and scraping the bottom with a heat-proof spatula, until the custard thickens. Add liquor, vanilla, and cinnamon, if using.
- Chill the mixture for about 5 hours. Once thoroughly chilled, add the remaining half-and-half and blend. Pour into ice cream maker. Add the bacon bits during the last moment of churning, or stir them in when you remove the ice cream from the machine. Enjoy!

Coolhaus

Christine Aldrich and Nathan Hathaway were friends for many years and partners in life before picking up the torch for Coolhaus, a "choose your own ice cream and cookie" adventure in the trailer food business, in early 2010. In a merging of food and architecture, Nathan made the 1984 vintage mail truck from Los Angeles what it is today. With a background in food and a love for baking, Christine manages the flavors that are as nontraditional as they are delicious. Their favorite items on the menu include mascarpone and balsamic fig on snickerdoodle and coffee toffee on a chocolate cookie. Rest assured; many hours of quality control have gone into choosing the items on their superfine menu.

Midnight Moons

Courtesy of Gonzo Juice

Here is a recipe for some homemade Oreos—make as many layers as you want.

1 cup heavy whipping cream
1 teaspoon sugar
¼ teaspoon vanilla
Nabisco Famous Chocolate
  Wafers

- Whip cream, sugar, and vanilla until thick, closer to the consistency of butter.

- Scoop 1 ounce portions between two wafers and let settle in fridge for 6 to 8 hours before serving.

Index

Photography Index